MINI POWER TOOL
Handbook

Zachary Taylor & Colin Bullock

Sterling Publishing Co., Inc.
New York

Library of Congress Cataloging-in-Publication Data

Taylor, Zachary
  Mini power tool handbook/Zachary Taylor & Colin Bullock.
    p. cm.
  ISBN 0-8069-2292-3
  1. Power tools—Handbooks, manuals, etc. I. Bullock, Colin. II. Title.

TJ1195 .T39 2002
621.9—dc21

2001055060

1 3 5 7 9 10 8 6 4 2

Published by Sterling Publishing Company, Inc.
387 Park Avenue South, New York, N.Y. 10016
© 2002 by Zachary Taylor and Colin Bullock
Distributed in Canada by Sterling Publishing
℅ Canadian Manda Group, One Atlantic Avenue, Suite 105
Toronto, Ontario, Canada M6K 3E7
Distributed in Great Britain and Europe by Cassell PLC
Wellington House, 125 Strand, London WC2R OBB, England
Distributed in Australia by Capricorn Link (Australia) Pty. Ltd.
P.O. Box 704, Windsor, NSW 2756, Australia
Printed in China
Sterling ISBN 0-8069-2292-3

This book is dedicated to 'Tricia and Rosie,
with thanks for the support and forbearance with the "toys for the boys" and a lot of love.
Zachary and Colin

Acknowledgments

Several people helped in various ways to make this book possible. Thanks are due from the authors to: Richard Lenthall of Robert Bosch Ltd., for the supply of Dremel products; Fredrik Jacobsson of Macford Products Ltd., for the supply of Minicraft products; Arturo Martorelli of Black & Decker, for the supply of Wizard products; Martin Brown of BriMarc Associates, for the supply of Proxxon products; Record Tools, for the supply of Quick-Grip clamps; Ken Edge and Glyn Billson of Chesterman Marketing, for the supply of Jorgensen clamps.

Photographs throughout this book are by Colin Bullock

CONTENTS

Chapter Three

ROUTING   45

ROUTING ATTACHMENTS   47

INLAYING TECHNIQUES   62

THE ROUTING TABLE   65

Chapter Four

SAWING & CUTTING TECHNIQUES   72

ACCESSORIES DEDICATED TO SAWING OPERATIONS   77

Chapter Five
FLEXIBLE DRIVES

Chapter Six
SHAPING AND SMOOTHING

INTRODUCTION

A range of mini power tools has emerged over the past few years that has established itself firmly in the essential toolbox of model makers, craftspeople, woodworkers, and DIY enthusiasts (**I–1**). The ability of these tools to produce fine, precise results combined with the versatility of a wide range of accessories has made them a perfect complement to the bigger power tools.

While precision is always a function of the operator's skill, mini power tools certainly make such work easier. Whereas standard power tools have cutters whose diameter is measured in inches and 10's of millimeters, mini power tool cutters rarely exceed .20 inch (5 mm). High-speed, lightweight motors in a molded case designed to be handheld reduce the tendency of cutters to kick back and allow the user to produce precision work.

Most full-size power tools are dedicated to one task, for example, drilling, sawing, or routing. Mini power tools offer superb versatility by offering a wide range of cutters and add-on accessories, which means they can be turned to virtually any area of precision work. These accessories are available in convenient bubble packs, and are sold either individually or as part of a collection advertised for furniture restoration, home improvement, or car detailing. The work they are capable of doing includes carving, engraving, and model making. (Small-sized cutters

I–1. Selection of mini power tools.

and abrasives are ideal for working in confined spaces or for delicate, small-scale work.) The range of operations that can be performed includes drilling, routing, shaping, smoothing, polishing, engraving, and sawing. Even the range of materials that can be worked is widely varied, and includes wood, plastic, metal, glass, stone, and ceramics.

In addition to the range of cutters and abrasives, most systems offer router guides, drill stands, flexible drives, bench stands, and other special attachments that extend the usefulness of the basic tool, turning it into a miniature workshop (**I–2**).

Many manufacturers offer a range of dedicated units designed for specific tasks (**I–3**). These avoid the need to dismantle or change attachments when moving from one operation to another. This is especially useful for repetitive sequences of operations as settings can be maintained during different parts of the process.

I–2. Range of attachments for the mini power tool. Shown are a router table, router base, and drill stand.

I–3. Dedicated units for a mini power tool include a saw table, disc sander, jigsaw, and orbital sander.

SELECTING A MINI POWER TOOL

The mini power tool selected will depend upon the type of use to which it will be put and hence the range of attachments that the user feels will be necessary for the tasks to be performed. Chapters 2 to 8 give detailed information on the range of equipment available, and **Table 1** on pages 135 to 137 lists the specifications and attachments available for specific models. Here we will discuss the general types of mini power tool. **Table I–1** on page 12 lists these types and their primary uses.

Power

Mini power tools are powered by a main circuit (110 or 240 volts), a transformer (at a low voltage, usually 12 volts), or by batteries, including rechargeable types. Each system has its advantages and disadvantages, as discussed below.

Main-Circuit Power

Main-circuit-powered mini power tools (**I–4**) conveniently use any main-circuit electrical socket. They tend to be heavier for comparable power and, although more expensive than a single low-voltage unit, the total cost is usually less, because they need no low-voltage transformer. This lack of a separate transformer makes them more portable, particularly for DIY operations around the house. Currently, all the available systems have a comprehensive range of accessories and attachments.

Low-Voltage Mini Power Tools

Low-voltage mini power tools (**I–5**) are lighter and it is necessary to connect them to the main-circuit power through a transformer. Some transformers incorporate facilities to connect several units simultaneously, thus offering lower costs overall when compared with the main-circuit-powered types. As they work on low power (less than 24 volts), some makes are useable in wet or damp conditions, for example, wet-and-dry sanding—although care must be taken to keep the power unit dry and to protect it with a Ground Fault Circuit Interrupter, also known as a RCD (residual current detector). (Check the manufacturer's instructions to see if a particular unit is suitable.)

I–4. Main-circuit-powered mini power tool.

I–5. A low-volt mini power tool.

I–6. Rechargeable mini power tool.

The speed of the mini power tool is usually controlled by an adjustment available on the transformer, although some less-expensive transformers have only a single speed. Because of the separate transformer, low-voltage units are best suited to work where the unit is not carried from one place to another, for example, on a workbench.

Because many units are powered by 12 volts, they have the option of being connected to a car battery and can therefore be used away from the workshop.

Rechargeable Battery-Powered Mini Power Tools

These tools (**I–6**) are more portable than the other types, as they do not rely on a main-circuit electrical socket. They are safe in damp and wet conditions and lightweight, but they are less powerful and often have less speed variation than the other main-circuit-powered tools. Battery life is also a consideration, as they have an annoying habit of running out at the least convenient time, so always keep a spare battery fully charged.

Some battery-powered units cannot be connected to attachments and are therefore not suitable for operations such as routing.

Dedicated Flexible-Drive and Engraving Mini Power Tools

If working mainly at a bench on tasks such as carving and engraving, the user may wish to consider a dedicated flexible-drive mini power tool that incorporates the on/off switch and speed control on a foot-powered unit. (Refer to **I–7** and Chapter 5.) The hand piece on these units is also lighter than that of other mini power tools; this produces less strain on the hands during extended use and makes the unit easier to control for finer work.

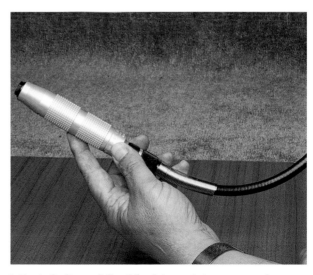

I–7. A dedicated flexible drive mini power tool.

Although flexible-drive attachments are available for most mini power tools, they are not as versatile as the dedicated unit. Also, the period of use is often limited as they lack the ball-bearing systems of the dedicated unit and can run considerably hotter, causing discomfort to the user.

For sole use on engraving, there are also dedicated engraving units that are especially light for extended use and incorporate an on/off switch under the user's index finger, for ease of control (**I–8**).

I–8. **Engraving glass using a dedicated engraving unit.**

Table I–1.

TYPE OF MINI POWER TOOL	PRIMARY USE
Main-Circuit	DIY Bench use with attachments
Low voltage	Bench use
Battery-Powered	Portable
Flexible Drive	Carving and engraving
Engraver	Engraving only

chapter

One

GETTING STARTED

PARTS OF A MINI POWER TOOL

Someone using a mini power tool for the first time should become familiar with its parts. Illus.

1–1 to 1–11 show the typical parts of a mini power tool.

MINI POWER TOOL PARTS AND FEATURES

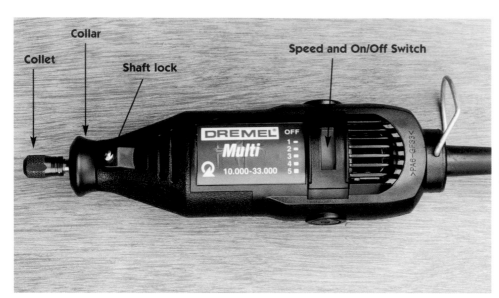

Collar

Collet

Shaft lock

Speed and On/Off Switch

DREMEL
Multi
10.000-33.000
OFF
1
2
3
4
5

1–1. A look at the different parts of a mini power tool.

1–2. The collet or chuck is used to hold rotary cutters and drill bits. Here a collet is shown attached to the mini power tool, and below it is a chuck.

1–3. In order to aid the fitting of accessories, most mini power tools have a shaft or spindle lock, usually in the form of a small button. When depressed, the lock prevents the spindle from rotating when changing a collet or chuck, when fitting an accessory.

1–4. Many mini power tools when held like a pencil are shaped to suit the fingers.

1–5. Most mini power tools have a removable collar where the spindle emerges. This unscrews to reveal a thread, which can then be used to fit various attachments. Alternatively, the collar may be replaced with a different type that acts as an adapter when fitting attachments.

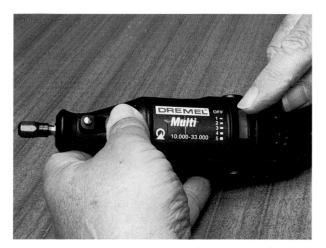

1–6. This type of mini power tool has a combined on/off switch and speed control.

1–7. Here a continuously variable speed is set by rotating the knob.

1–8. This mini power tool has a separate trigger-type on/off switch.

1–10. The choice of speed in revolutions per minute of this mini power tool is adjusted by depressing one of the two lower buttons on the rear of the unit. To increase or decrease the rpm, depress the right or left button, respectively. The resultant rpm is shown in the small screen above the two buttons.

1–9. Most low-voltage mini power tools have the speed control on the power transformer. If there is a speed control on the mini power tool, then the transformer is set to full power or a fixed-voltage transformer is used.

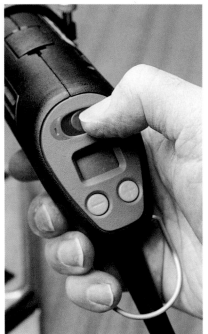

1–11. Above the small screen is located the on/off power switch.

SAFETY MEASURES

As with all power tools, the safety of the user and passersby is paramount. Mini power tools are not inherently dangerous and a few simple guidelines will suffice to avoid personal injury. Illus. **1–12 to 1–17** show safety procedures when using a mini power tool. Also follow these prudent measures:

1. It is important to get into a safety routine, a standard procedure to follow every time the mini power tool is used. Before changing tool bits or accessories, do not only switch off the tool but also disconnect it from the main-circuit power supply. Always make sure the unit is switched off before connecting it to the main-circuit supply. Then set the speed and switch on the tool.

2. Remember, mini power tools are not toys; do not allow unsupervised children to use them.

3. When running a mini power tool, be aware of the sound of the motor. When the machine is running without load, notice the pitch of the motor as an audible guide. If the pitch of the motor drops when applying a cut or any other work load, or if the mini power tool appears to be straining, release the pressure on the tool so that the speed can return close to the no-load speed. Straining a motor will result in overheating and early wear of the mini power tool, shortening its working life.

4. Check the manufacturer's instructions to see if there is a maximum "continuous-use" time. Do not exceed this time and, if the machine is used to the full duration of its recommended time, remember to allow the mini power tool to cool before using it again.

SAFETY PROCEDURES

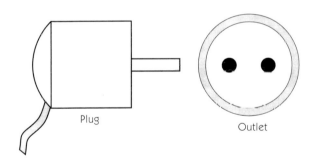

1–12. Disconnect the tool before changing tool bits or accessories; do not only switch off the tool, but also disconnect it from the main-circuit power supply. Check that the tool is switched off before plugging in the power cord (cable).

1–13. Keep a firm grip on the tool. Keep the workpiece firmly supported. If a vise is being used, best to fix it securely by screws to the worktop.

1–14. When changing cutters, it is sensible to wear gloves for protection of the fingers from sharp edges. Leather gloves such as used for gardening or gloves made of similar strong material are recommended.

1–15. Keep fingers away from the cutters. Always use the guards provided.

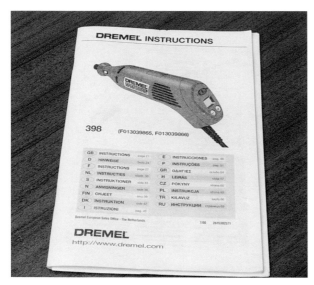

1–16. Follow the manufacturer's instructions—read the manual.

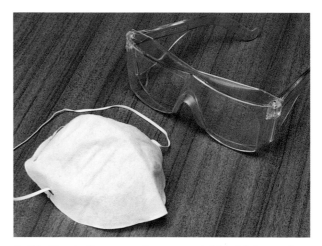

1–17. Dust of any sort is a potential health hazard; the most dangerous dust is too small to be seen by the naked eye. Therefore, respiration should be protected by the use of masks, many varieties of which are available. Also, protection for the eyes—either safety glasses or goggles—should be worn.

Illus. **1–18** to **1–21** show the setup for mini power tools using main-circuit power, transformers, and batteries.

SETTING UP THE MINI POWER TOOL

1–18. Mini power tools using main-circuit power connect directly to the main-circuit power and will incorporate the on/off switch and speed control on the unit.

1–19. Low-voltage units plug into a transformer that will be either single speed or incorporate a speed controller. Some transformers have multiple connectors to allow more than one mini power tool to be connected at the same time. The power rating of the transformer will determine whether more than one unit can be run at the same time. If the output voltage of the transformer is 100V, for example, it will accept just about any tool available at the moment. Other transformers are available with lower outputs of 24 and 12V, and these are suitable to drive the smaller machines. Reference to the technical information contained on the power labels of the equipment should indicate this.

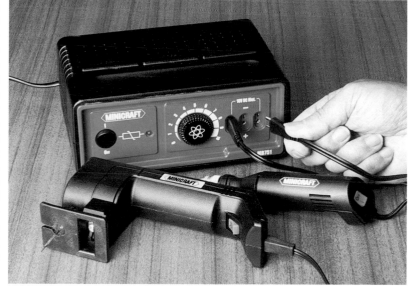

1–21. Battery-powered units will need a disposable set of batteries of the proper voltage or a battery that is rechargeable.

Do not recharge the battery after using it for a short time; always use it until the battery is discharged. This is because some rechargeable batteries—for example, NiCad batteries—tend to develop a memory effect that limits their efficiency if they are not fully discharged before recharging. If this happens, the effect can be corrected by charging the battery and then discharging it by running the mini power tool until it slows down. Repeat this full discharge at least three times.

Most recent rechargeables—for example, NiMh batteries—do not exhibit this effect.

If the mini power tool is not used for some time, the batteries tend to discharge themselves, so it is best to check at least one hour before starting work that the batteries have power and, if necessary, recharge them.

1–20. Some transformers incorporate an overload device that will detect if too much power is being consumed and prevent damage to the transformer. If this device activates, switch off the mini power tool, disconnect the transformer from the main-circuit power, and allow it to cool for a while before trying to reset the overload button. Some units have an automatic overload reset that will detect when the transformer has cooled and allow it to restart when the power is switched on again.

HOLDING CUTTERS AND OTHER ROTATING TOOLS

Cutters and other rotating tools may be held in either a collet or a chuck. Illus. **1–22 to 1–29** show the use of collets and **1–30 to 1–32** demonstrate a chuck.

INSERTING CUTTERS IN COLLETS

1–22. A close-up of a collet and its parts. A collet has inner jaws that hold the drill or cutter firmly in place. It is a very secure way of holding cutters because of its precise diameter that matches the diameter of the shank of the cutter. This reduces vibration caused by side play when applying a cutting action. There are, however, a limited range of collet sizes available and the cutter shank has to be within a close tolerance of the collet size in order to grip firmly. Most cutters and arbors are ⅛ inch (3.2 mm) in diameter, with some larger ones with a ¼-inch (6.4-mm) diameter available. The collet should be the preferred means of holding cutters and accessories on arbors. (See 1–30 to 1–32 for details on using chucks.)

Collet nuts usually feature a knurled surface to facilitate secure gripping with the fingers. In addition, there will be a flat, on either side, to permit the use of a wrench (spanner) for maximizing the grip of the collet. The wrench should be used with discretion because overtightening could distort the collet, rendering it insecure and therefore potentially dangerous.

Most manufacturers offer a range of collet sizes, usually to hold shank diameters from .020 to .126 inch (0.5 to 3.2 mm).

1–23. It is sometimes necessary to change the collet to suit a particular diameter of a cutter shaft. This is done by removing the threaded collet nut and withdrawing the unwanted collet. Having selected the correct collet to suit the chosen shaft, it is inserted into the spindle and the collet nut is replaced and tightened.

1–24. When changing a drill bit or other cutter, it is necessary to release it by loosening the collet. When applying the unscrewing motion to the collet, it is necessary to lock the spindle of the mini power tool; this is achieved by temporarily depressing the spindle lock and rotating the spindle until the lock engages. To enable cutter changes, all mini power tools are fitted with a spindle lock, usually operated by the depressing of a button placed conveniently near the end of the spindle. Under no circumstances should the shaft lock be engaged while the mini power tool is running. Do not engage it while the mini power tool is connected to the power source, in case it is switched on accidentally.

1–25. When fitting the collet, unscrew the collet nut completely and remove it from the spindle. Insert the collet into the open end of the spindle and replace the collet nut.

1–28. Put as much of the shank into the collet as is possible and, holding down the shaft lock, tighten the collet nut to finger tight.

1–26. To place a cutter in the collet, first switch off and disconnect the mini power tool. Depress the shaft lock and loosen the collet nut.

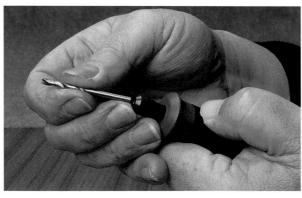

1–27. Insert the cutter or drill bit. If force is required, unscrew the collet nut more until the cutter can be inserted with no feeling of resistance.

1–29. If more pressure is needed to tighten the collet nut, apply the wrench—but with care. (See 1–22.)

INSERTING CUTTERS IN CHUCKS

1–30. A very adaptable accessory is a chuck, which is an alternative to the collet. The three jaws incorporated in the chuck are infinitely adjustable in diameter from about .04 to .20 inch (1 to 5 mm). Because of its variable-grip diameter, the chuck is flexible in its ability to accept cutters of various shank diameter, but it cannot hold as efficiently as a collet and cutter with matching diameters. Chucks are best used with small-diameter drill bits.

Fitting a chuck to the mini power tool is very straightforward. Remove the collet nut and the collet, and then fit the chuck by screwing it onto the spindle. Remember, it is necessary to depress the shaft lock when adding or removing these parts.

1–31. To place a cutter in the chuck, first switch off and disconnect the mini power tool. On this type of mini power tool, the shaft lock is a knurled ring that is held between the thumb and forefinger while the other hand loosens the chuck body to open the jaws until the drill shank slides in.

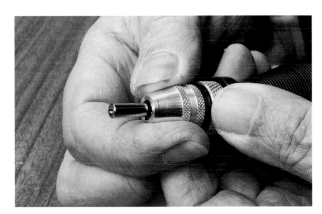

1–32. Insert as much of the shank into the chuck as is possible and, holding down the shaft lock, tighten the chuck as much as possible with the fingers.

HOLDING THE WORK AND TOOLS

A firm grip on the tool and workpiece will help prevent mishap. Holding a small workpiece in one hand and the tool in the other will often result in injury if one or other skids/moves. Ideally, clamp the workpiece in a vise or to a workbench. With the workpiece firmly held, both hands can be applied to controlling the mini power tool.

There are a number of useful grips that can be employed. Illus. **1–33 to 1–37** show one-handed grips. Illus **1–38 to 1–41** show two-handed grip positions.

Most mini power tools have a stand that can be used to hold them in a variety of positions. Illus. **1–42 to 1–52** show how to attach this stand to the workbench.

It is important during drilling operations that the workpiece be held firmly in position. Illus. **1–53 to 1–56** show how to accomplish this using a vise or clamps.

ONE-HANDED GRIPS

1–33. Overhand grip (similar to a grip on a motorcycle handlebar) on the tool with fingers curved over the top of the tool and the thumb underneath. The thumb can be rested on a firm surface to give support.

1–34. Tennis style underhand grip. It is useful for drilling horizontally.

1–35. Stabbing grip.

1–36. The design of some mini power tools is suitable for a pistol grip.

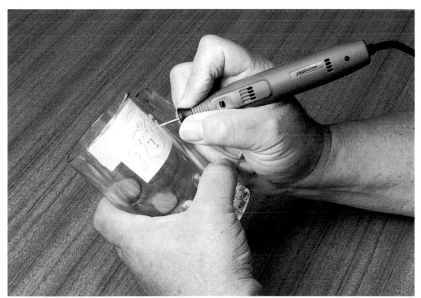

1–37. Pencil grip used mainly for engraving and polishing detail.

TWO-HANDED GRIPS

1–38. Two-handed grips give extra stability. An underhand–overhand combination gives firm support. This grip is particularly useful for grinding, sanding, and polishing.

1–39. It can be useful to rest the fingers of one hand on a firm surface to increase the fine control.

1–40. If held as shown here, the cutter or abrasive disc can throw dust or particles toward the eyes of the user.

1–41. The proper way to hold a mini power tool is to allow dust or other particles to be directed away from the operator.

ATTACHING A STAND TO THE WORKBENCH

1–42. Most mini power tools have an accessory that can be used to hold the mini power tool in either a horizontal...

1–43. ...or a vertical position.

1–44. The stand often comes as a set of parts that need assembling. This is a very simple operation if the correct sequence is followed.

1–45. The securing bolt is inserted through one of the position-clamping brackets.

1–46. The pivot of the collar is positioned in the clamping brackets.

1–49. The securing nut is then inserted.

1–47. The bottom lug of the bracket is fitted into the main clamp body.

1–48. The other bracket is inserted.

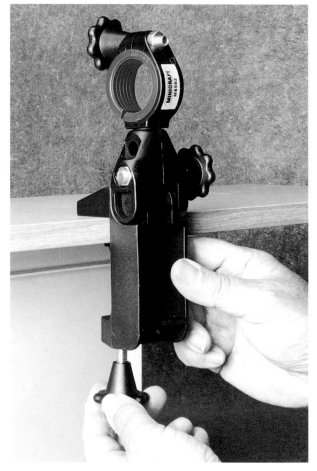

1–50. The complete assembly can then be secured to the workbench.

1–51. The adapter collar (if required) is placed over the mini power tool body, taking care not to obstruct the ventilation vents. The mini power tool is then inserted into the clamp.

1–52. The locking nut is then tightened to hold the mini power tool firmly in place.

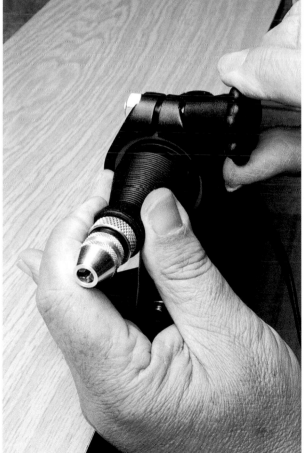

ACCESSORIES FOR HOLDING THE WORKPIECE IN PLACE

1–53. A small vise is a useful accessory for holding small items.

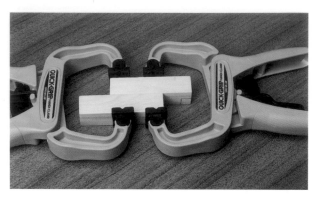

1–54. Clamps such as these can be used to hold work onto a bench or hold several parts together. The scissor action allows single-handed operation while positioning the work with the other.

1–55. These bar clamps are also for single-handed use and can hold either work or accessories in place.

1–56. Larger versions are available to hold projects in place.

chapter

DRILLING

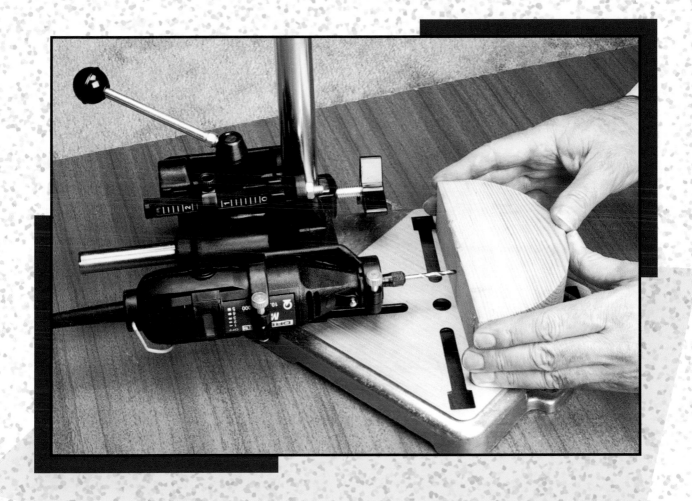

Drilling can be performed using either twist drill bits or bottom-cut router bits (**2–1**). The name "bottom-cut bit" means that its design incorporates a cutting face at the end, as well as at the side, of the cutter, permitting it to serve as a drill. Router bits are only recommended for use on wood and are best fitted in a collet rather than a chuck, as they all have a standard shank diameter. High-speed-steel twist drills can be used on wood, metal, and plastic, but because the shank is usually the same diameter as the drill and many diameters are available, they are usually mounted in a chuck.

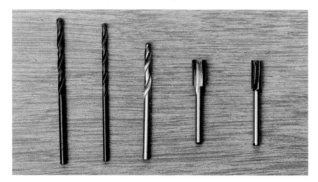

2–1. Bottom-cut router bits and twist drill bits.

Twist drills have a pointed tip that can help to position the drill over the center of the mark. They have spiral flutes that help to clear waste material (swarf) from the hole.

Router bits are described in Chapter 4. The type of router bits used for drilling have a flat bottom with cutting edges on both the bottom and sides. If they are not used to drill completely through the material, they will produce a flat-bottomed hole.

The illustrations in this chapter depict a variety of drilling techniques, including: ways to prevent drill-bit slippage and splintering (**pages 32 and 33**); methods for drilling holes in small workpieces (**pages 34 to 38**); how to attach the mini power tool to a drill stand and use it to more easily drill holes (**pages 38 to 42**); freehand drilling (**pages 42 to 44**); and the use of flexible-drive attachments and router bases (**page 44**).

PREVENTING DRILL-BIT SLIPPAGE

2–2. On hard materials with a smooth surface, for example, metal or plastic, the drill bit is likely to skid away from the mark as the drilling operation commences. This can be avoided by creating an indent in the surface of the workpiece to locate the center of the hole to prevent drill-bit slippage. A tool called a center punch may be used for this job. Having positioned the point of the center punch on the mark of the hole center, a smart tap with a hammer produces the required indent.

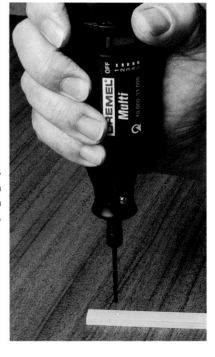

2–3. The drill-bit tip will then locate easily in the indentation.

2–4. Alternatively, if no center punch is available, a piece of masking tape may be placed in the position intended for the hole with its center marked with a pencil. This should help to locate the drill bit and prevent it slipping as it enters the surface of the material.

WASTE MATERIAL AND SPLINTERING

2–5. Drilling operations create waste material that is ejected through the flutes incorporated in the drill bit; this waste is commonly called "swarf." On holes deeper than ¼ inch (6 mm), it is important to withdraw the drill occasionally to clear swarf from the drill flutes, to prevent clogging and overheating of the drill.

2–6. It is not advisable to drill to a depth greater than the drill flutes because the waste material cannot escape and this would risk overheating, blockage of the flutes, and subsequent damage.

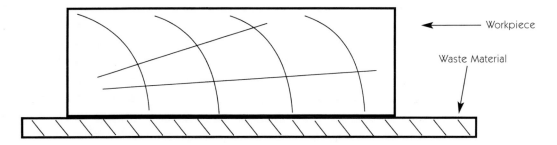

Workpiece

Waste Material

2–7. When drilling right through the material, proceed slowly when the drill is about to break through the bottom of the work, to help prevent splintering. Often a piece of waste material, for example, wood, placed under the workpiece will prevent splintering when the drill breaks through.

DRILLING HOLES IN SMALL WORKPIECES

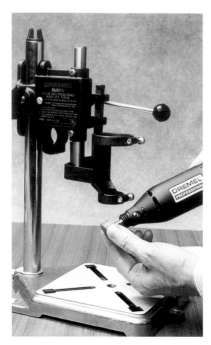

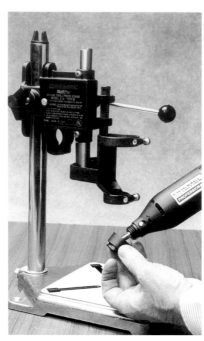

2–8. Drilling holes in small work-pieces is best performed with the work held in a vise and drilled with the mini power tool held securely in a drill-stand accessory. To mount the mini power tool in the drill stand, it may be necessary to change the collar on the nose of the mini power tool or use an adapter ring. First, remove the collar, as shown here.

2–9. Replace the collar with the adapter.

2–10. When the mini power tool is being attached to the drill stand, it should be arranged so that the shaft lock should be accessible.

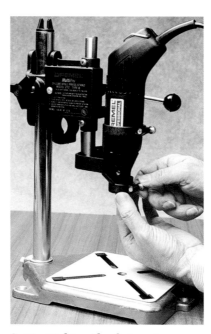

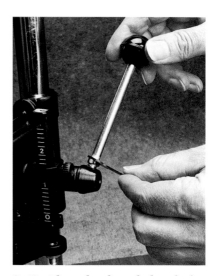

2–11. Tighten the fixing rings around the collar or body of the mini power tool.

2–12. Place the threaded end of the lever into the hole provided and use the small wrench to tighten it for security.

2–13. Insert the drill bit into the chuck or collet. In this example, a drill bit of a correct diameter is used to fit the collet.

2–14. Holding down the shaft lock with the thumb, tighten the chuck or collet to secure the drill bit.

2–15. Still holding down the shaft lock, the wrench may be used to firmly tighten the collet. Do not overtighten, as this may strain the collet parts.

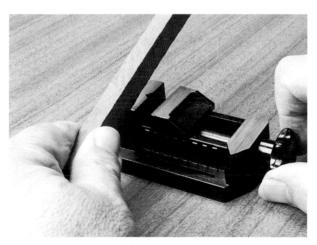

2–16. Secure the workpiece in a vise...

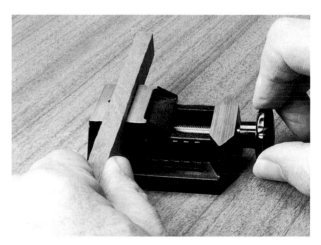

2–17. ...and tighten the clamping knob.

2–18. Alternatively, the workpiece may be held firm against a fence clamped directly onto the drill table.

2–19. The fence clamps are kept at the correct height using packing blocks at the rear.

2–20. Check the distance from the fence to the position of the drill bit.

2–21. Ensure that the drill is so located as to go through the hole in the center of the table. In this way, it will not drill into the table and mark the surface.

2–22. The workpiece is then set up against the fence and the column lock loosened to allow the drill to be approximately 3/8 inch (9 mm) above the work surface.

2–23. The control lever is then used to lower the drill and produce the required hole.

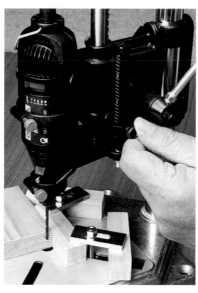

2–24. For drilling a blind hole—that is, one that does not go completely through the workpiece—the depth stop should be set to the required depth. In this case, use the lever to lower the drill onto the work to check it is on the mark. The drill bit is lowered onto the workpiece with the mini power tool switched off.

2–25. Check that the depth setting is correct before drilling the hole.

2–26. For repetition drilling, it is possible to mark a series of reference points on the fence. The work is then moved to the next mark for each consecutive hole as shown in 2–27 to 2–30.

2–27. The first hole is drilled with the end of the workpiece up against the first mark.

2–28. The end of the work is moved to the next pencil mark and the second hole is drilled.

2–29. This process is continued for subsequent holes...

2–30. ...until a series of equally spaced holes has been drilled.

2–32. Relocation of the clamping screw is necessary to secure the head in its horizontal position.

CHANGING THE ORIENTATION OF THE HOLDER

2–31. With certain drill stands, it is possible to change the orientation of the mini power tool holder (we will call it the "head"), in order to more easily drill a workpiece from the side. To achieve this, the head is first removed from the drill-stand column.

2–33. After the clamping screw is relocated, the head is slid onto the drill-stand column and fixed in position by tightening the clamping screw.

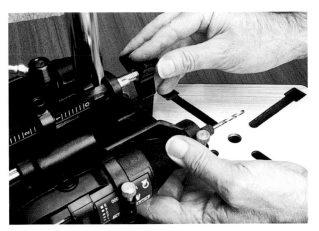

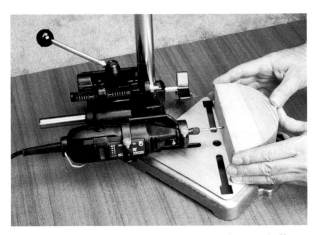

2–34. To obtain optimum efficiency, the head may be rotated on the column as well as located at the correct height to perform the drilling operation.

2–35. With the mini power tool correctly set, drilling can commence with both hands controlling the workpiece. If a depth stop is required, it is a simple matter to clamp a small block of wood onto the table of the drill stand to limit the travel of the workpiece.

ATTACHING THE MINI POWER TOOL TO A DRILL STAND

2–36. A very simple system for attaching the mini power tool to a drill stand is available with this model. Having made sure that the collar on the drill head is loosened, insert the mini power tool.

2–37. Make sure that the mini power tool is seated firmly in the collar and tighten the clamping screw.

2–38. To adjust the drill head to the height required for the drilling operation, slide it to the correct position on the column and then secure it by tightening the clamping screw.

2–39. A more sophisticated stand is available that requires assembly of the kit parts shown.

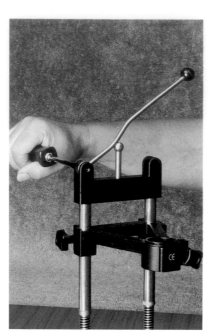

2–40. The control lever is positioned and secured with a small screw.

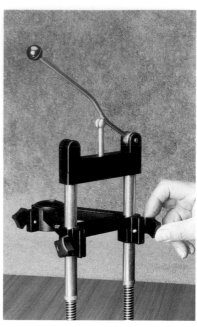

2–41. Clamping screws are used to secure the height of the column.

2–42. A clamping screw is inserted into the holder that will secure the mini power tool.

2–43. Depending on the model of mini power tool, an adapter may be required; this adapter will be supplied with the stand.

2–44. The mini power tool fitted with the appropriate adapter is inserted into the holder...

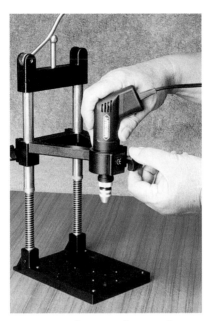

2–45. ... and secured using the clamping screw.

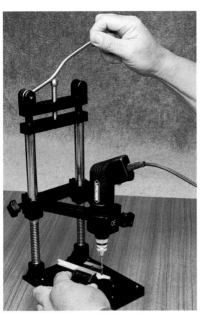

2–46. In use, the lever pushes the drill down into the workpiece.

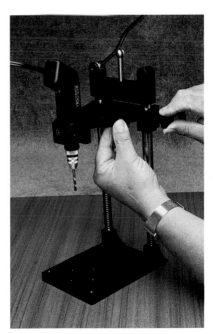

2–47. It is possible to adjust the height of the mini power tool on the column as shown, using the two clamping screws.

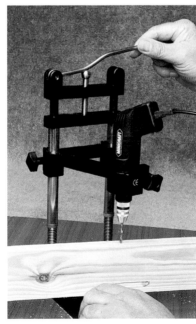

2–48. This allows larger workpieces to be accommodated.

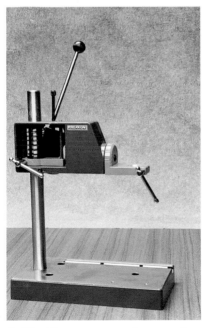

2–49. The system used to attach this mini power tool is similar to the one used for the model shown in 2–36 to 2–48.

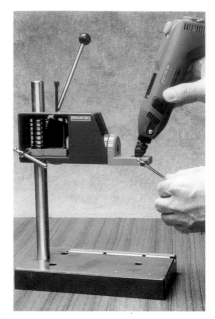

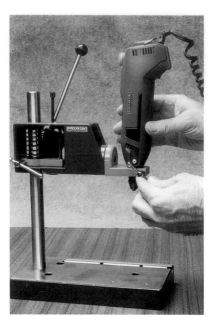

2–50. This mini power tool is primarily located by insertion into the aperture provided in the drill head. Make sure that the aperture is opened sufficiently to receive the collar on the mini power tool. This model does not have a removable collar, but some may require a size adapter to be fastened over the collar to allow fitting to the stand. Any such adapters are usually supplied with the stand.

2–51. Clamp the mini power tool in position after seating it firmly in the clamp.

2–52. It is possible to control the depth of the hole to be drilled by presetting the depth stop provided in this model. This mini power tool is especially suited to repetitive drilling operations.

FREEHAND DRILLING

2–53. When freehand drilling, care must be taken to keep the drill bit perpendicular to the work surface and avoid excessive pressure, as the drill bit is likely to bend due to its small diameter.

2–54. A stabbing grip may be used for vertical drilling.

2–55. A tennis-style grip can be used for horizontal freehand drilling.

2–56. Guide blocks and squares can be used to help keep the drill vertical. The simple L-shaped block shown here has been made to help control the perpendicular progress of the drill bit when drilling.

2–57. These guides are easily made using a small block of wood marked with a pencil and square as shown. It is important to ensure that the section to be removed has its sides and faces at 90 degrees to each other.

2–58. The first cut is made with a saw—in this case, a mini power tool jigsaw.

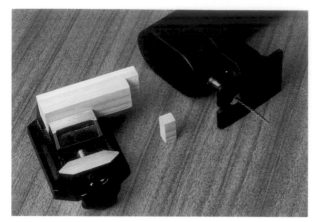

2–59. A second cut is taken at right angles to remove the corner piece to form the guide block.

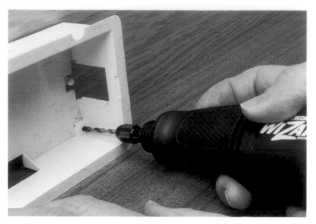

2–60. The mini power tool may also be used free-hand for DIY drilling, for example, fastening fixtures to a ceiling or wall. Its light weight makes it ideal for use in such situations.

USING FLEXIBLE-DRIVE ATTACHMENTS AND ROUTER BASES

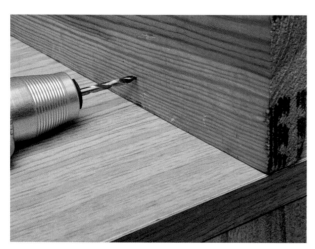

2–61. Most mini power tools can also be fitted with a flexible-drive attachment. This is especially useful for drilling in confined spaces.

2–62. When the workpiece is larger than can be accommodated on the drill stand, it is possible to use a router attachment as an alternative to secure the mini power tool. This helps to keep the drill bit perpendicular and centered during the drilling operation. (See Chapter 3 for details on setup and use.) The router base is particularly useful for drilling holes in the edge of large panels.

three

ROUTING

Routers are used to cut grooves, moldings, and dadoes in both wood and some plastics. They can be used to produce simple toys and models, signs, and nameplates, as well as cutouts for inlay or intarsia.

Standard router bits made of high-speed steel (HSS) are suitable for routing wood and some soft plastics (**3–1 and 3–2**). They are available in a range of shapes and can be used to create various grooves and edge moldings (**3–3**). Bits made of tungsten carbide are also available (**3–4**). These bits are suit-able for wood, plastics, and, with care, metal.

For cutting without splintering the edges of the work, special downcut bits are available (**3–5**). The spiral on these bits forces the cutting edge down into the material with a shearing action that does not pull up or tear the surface. With some very soft wood, it may be necessary to score the edges of the cutting line to prevent splintering. This is done by scribing a line with a sharp blade before commencing to cut with the router.

TYPES OF ROUTER BIT

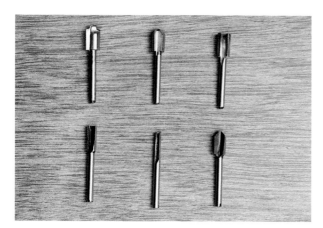

3–1. High-speed-steel standard router bits.

3–2. Pin-guided router bits.

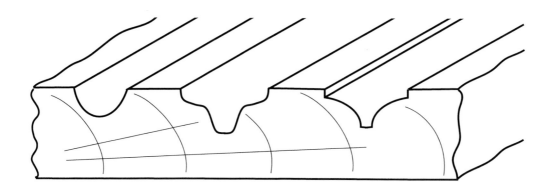

3–3. Shapes of cut produced with router bits.

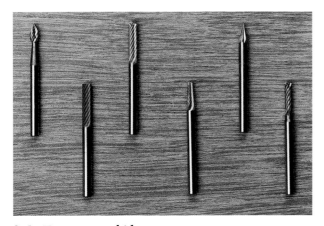

3–4. Tungsten-carbide cutters.

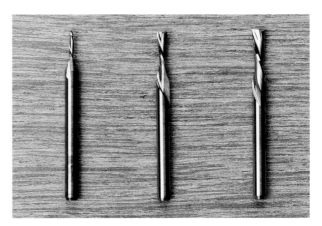

3–5. Downcut bits.

ROUTING ATTACHMENTS

Two basic types of attachment are available to convert the mini power tools for routing operations. They are a router base attachment and a router table. Illus. **3–6 to 3–19** show how to set up and use a router base attachment. Illus. **3–20 to 3–25** show how to use a router base attachment with a depth stop to fine-set the depth of cut. Illus. **3–26 to 3–40** depict how to use a router base for plunge routing, and **3–41 to 3–54** show miscellaneous routing techniques featuring a router base. Illus. **3–55 to 3–63** show inlaying techniques, and **3–64 and 3–65** depict techniques involving pin-guided bits.

Illus. **3–66 to 3–88** show techniques involving a router table.

SETTING UP A ROUTER BASE ATTACHMENT

3–6. The parts of the router base attachment are the base with handles, the fence with rods, and the adapter collar.

3–7. Fit the fence rods into the fence.

3–8. Tighten the wing nuts to hold the fence rods in place. Repeat for the other rod.

3–10. The fence can be slid toward or away from the body of the attachment...

3–9. Slide the fence rods into the router base and use a screwdriver to tighten the retaining screws.

3-11. ...to the required distance.

3–12. Install the mini power tool by fitting its collar into the clamping ring provided in the attachment. An adapter collar may be needed to fit the mini power tool correctly. In most cases, this would be supplied with the attachment.

3–13. Secure the mini power tool with the clamping screw in the collar.

3–14. Adjust the distance between the fence and the edge of the bit to suit the thickness of the workpiece and the finished width of cut.

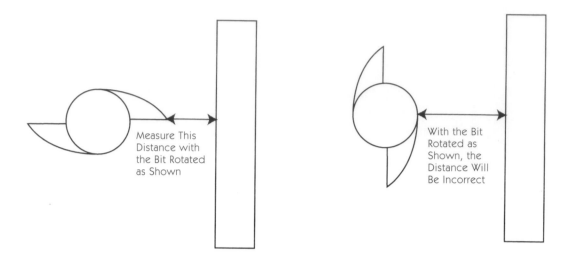

Measure This
Distance with
the Bit Rotated
as Shown

With the Bit
Rotated as
Shown, the
Distance Will
Be Incorrect

3–15. With most bits it is easier to measure from the fence to the edge of the bit. In this case, rotate the bit so that the cutting edge is closest to the fence; otherwise, a false measurement will result.

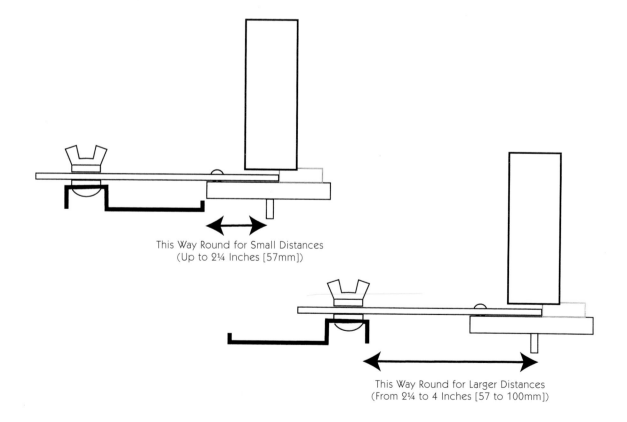

This Way Round for Small Distances
(Up to 2¼ Inches [57mm])

This Way Round for Larger Distances
(From 2¼ to 4 Inches [57 to 100mm])

3–16. With this model, it is possible to set the fence in two ways depending on the distance required.

3–17. Loosen the depth-adjustment lock...

3–18. ...and use the depth-adjustment screw to set the height of the cutter above the base.

3–19. Measure the bit projection as shown.

FINE-SETTING THE DEPTH OF CUT WITH A ROUTER BASE ATTACHMENT

3–20. If the router attachment incorporates a depth stop, this is a useful method for the fine setting of the depth of cut. In this case, the depth stop is moved to the correct position and locked by a screw to achieve the required depth of cut.

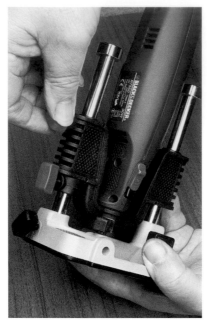

3–21. This base has a plunge facility that allows the mini power tool to be raised and lowered during the routing operation. It may also be used in a fixed position by the tightening of the locking screw on the plunging slide.

3–22. This routing attachment includes an adjustable fence.

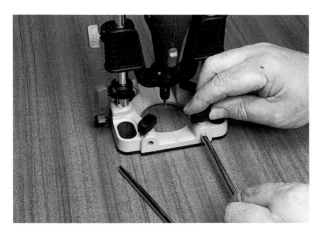

3–23. Fitting the fence rods and fixing them in position with the lock knobs.

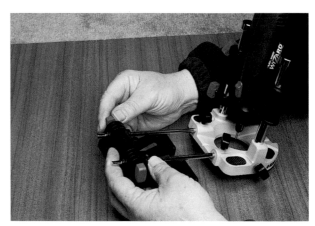

3–24. Providing the rods have been located and attached, their assembly into the body of the router attachment should be simple.

3–25. Here the router base is being used to provide secure perpendicular drilling of holes in a workpiece.

PLUNGE-ROUTING GROOVES

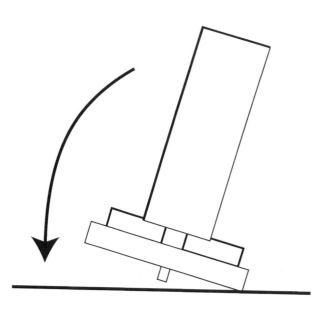

3–26. Some router attachments are designed for plunge routing. That is, when the base is placed on the work surface, the body of the router can be pushed down so that the bit enters the surface. This allows cuts to be made away from the edge of a workpiece. If a router attachment does not have a plunge facility, it is still possible to make shallow plunge cuts by angling the router base and pivoting the router bit into the work, as shown here.

3–27. Lightly mark each end of the groove using a pencil.

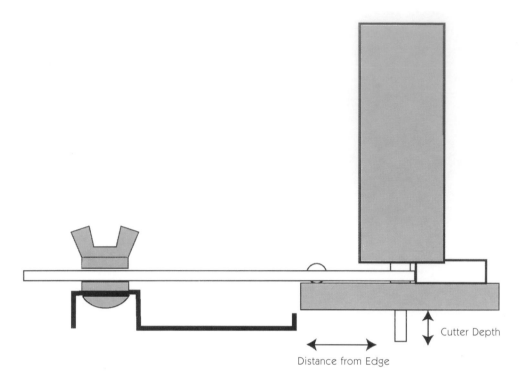

Cutter Depth

Distance from Edge

3–28. Set the fence to the required distance for the groove from the edge and the bit to the required depth of the groove.

3–29. Switch on the mini power tool to its highest speed. Place one edge of the router base in contact with the surface of the workpiece while keeping its opposite edge above the work surface to prevent contact with the bit.

3–30. Hold the fence firmly against the workpiece and gradually lower the router base until it rests fully on the surface of the workpiece. This, in effect, "plunges" the bit into the workpiece at the set depth and at the set distance from the edge of the workpiece. Take care to make this cut well into the waste area, as accidental side slip is possible.

3–31. Move the router base smoothly between the two pencil marks, keeping the fence firmly against the side of the work. Listen for any appreciable loss of speed that might indicate overloading the mini power tool. Reduce the rate of feed in this case. Also be aware that too slow a feed could result in over-heating the bit and cause burning to the workpiece and also the bit.

3–32. The fence keeps the bit at the required distance from the edge.

3–33. The finished groove.

PRESETTING THE DEPTH STOP USING A ROUTER BASE WITH PLUNGE AND DEPTH-STOP FACILITIES

3–34. A mini power tool fitted into a router base with plunge and depth-stop facilities.

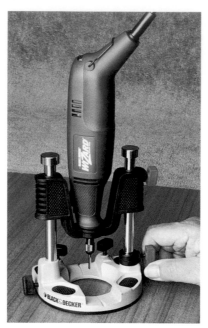

3–35. The retaining screw on the depth stop has been released, allowing it to rest on the base.

3–36. Here is shown the loosening of the locking screw in readiness for movement of the unit down the column.

3–37. The router has come to rest on the workbench top, and the retaining screw is tightened, temporarily preventing further movement of the unit on the column.

3–38. A strip of wood equal in thickness to the required routing depth is placed beneath the underside of the unit and the depth stop is drawn up to it. The depth-stop retaining screw is then tightened to hold it in that position.

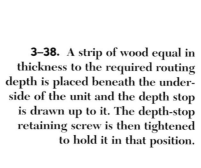

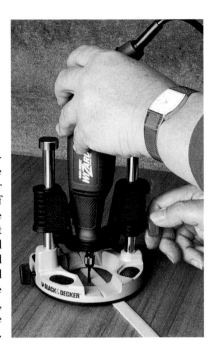

3–39. Releasing the column screw allows free movement of the mini power tool that now may be raised away from the workpiece or lowered into it. The depth stop will limit the downward travel of the router bit to the preset depth.

3–40. An alternative method of presetting the required position of the depth stop is as shown. The router base is placed on top of the strip of wood of the same thickness as the required depth of the router bit insertion. The depth stop is adjusted up to the bottom of the column and its retaining screw tightened to hold it in that position. Thus when the column is lowered to the depth stop, the router bit will penetrate the workpiece to the preset depth.

ROUTER MOVEMENT DIRECTION WHEN USING A BASE

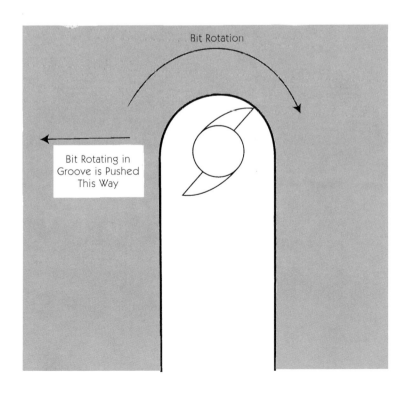

Bit Rotation

Bit Rotating in Groove is Pushed This Way

3–41. When cutting a groove in the middle of a piece of wood, the direction in which the router moves makes little difference. However, because of the tendency of the cutter or bit to pull in the direction shown, it is necessary to incorporate the use of the fence, to prevent the cutter deviating from the intended line of cut. When routing along an edge, however, only one side of the cutter touches the wood at any one time and it is important to understand what happens.

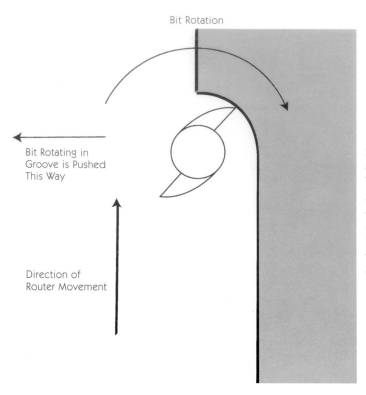

Bit Rotation

Bit Rotating in
Groove is Pushed
This Way

Direction of
Router Movement

3–42. Here the bit is seen from above rotating clockwise (as is normal). However, the cut is being made on the right-hand side of the bit and the cutter acts in two ways that would cause problems. First, as the cutting edge enters the wood it tends to push the bit away from the edge. Second, its action is similar to a wheel trying to drag the router along. This clearly is the wrong way to cut.

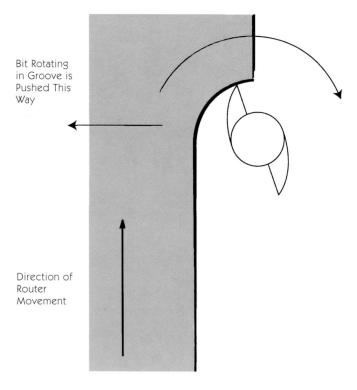

Bit Rotating in Groove is Pushed This Way

Direction of Router Movement

3–43. In this example, the edge is on the left of the bit (from the operator's perspective) and the action of the bit is to pull the router more firmly onto the edge. It clearly cannot be pulled off the correct line because the fence will keep it in position.

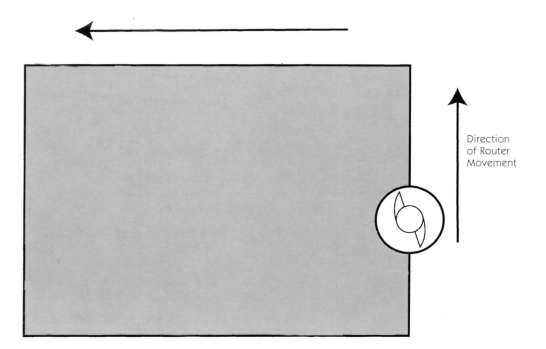

Direction
of Router
Movement

3–44. All this leads to two simple rules when using the router base. The first, as shown here, is that when cutting the outer edge of a piece of work, move the router around in a counterclockwise direction keeping the edge on the left of the base as it moves forward.

3–45. The second rule is that when routing a hole in the middle of a piece, move the router in the clockwise direction, again keeping the edge on the left of the router as it moves forward.

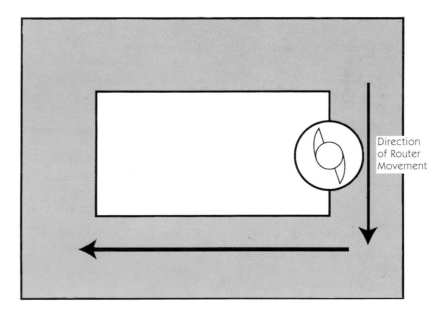

Direction
of Router
Movement

USING A ROUTER BASE WITH A SHOP-MADE FENCE

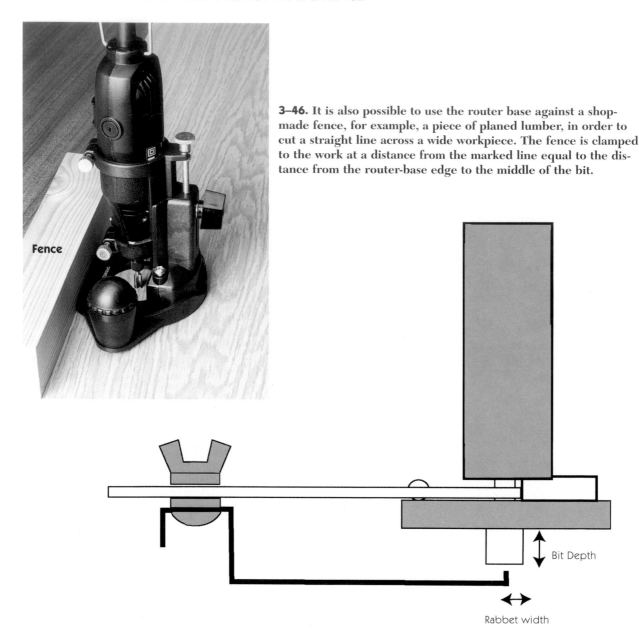

Fence

3–46. It is also possible to use the router base against a shop-made fence, for example, a piece of planed lumber, in order to cut a straight line across a wide workpiece. The fence is clamped to the work at a distance from the marked line equal to the distance from the router-base edge to the middle of the bit.

Bit Depth

Rabbet width

3–47. Routing a rabbet (rebate) along an edge with a fence. Having selected and fitted correctly the router bit, it is necessary to adjust two settings. One is the depth of the cut required, and this is adjusted by setting the router base at the correct distance above the bit. In effect, this is achieved by using the depth-setting or plunging operation to project the bit at the correct distance below the base. The second adjustment is for the width of the rabbet, and this is done by sliding the fence to a position related to the edge of the bit. This should correspond to the desired width of the rabbet.

CIRCLE-CUTTING TECHNIQUES

3–48. Some router bases have a circle-cutting feature on the fence. Putting a small nail through a hole in the fence allows the router base to be used in a similar way to a compass, cutting a circle with the bit.

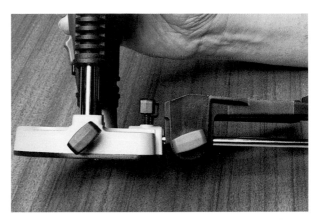

3–49. First, fit the fence in the circle-cutting mode.

3–50. Then drill a pilot hole the same diameter as the guide pin in the middle of the circle.

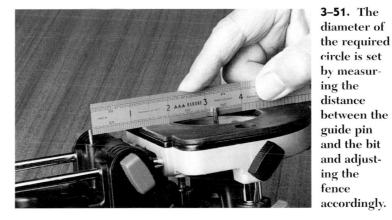

3–51. The diameter of the required circle is set by measuring the distance between the guide pin and the bit and adjusting the fence accordingly.

3–52. Insert the guide pin into the pilot hole.

3–53. The routing of the groove may now be performed using the assembly like a compass, rotating it around the pin in the middle of the circle.

3–54. Use a sanding tool to smooth the surface of the resulting groove.

INLAYING TECHNIQUES

Routers are often used to cut a cavity into a piece of wood so that a second piece can be inlayed into the surface. In this example shown in **3–55 to 3–63**, a heart-shaped piece of wood is inlayed.

INLAYING A HEART-SHAPED WOOD PIECE

3–55. A sharp-pointed pencil or other scribing tool may be used to mark the outline of the chosen shape for inlaying.

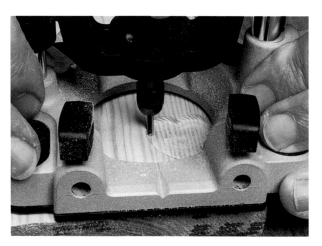

3–56. A small-diameter (preferably less than ¹⁄₁₆th inch [1.5 mm]), flat-bottomed bit is used to follow the detailed edge. The mini power tool is set to the same depth as the thickness of the piece to be inlaid. Switch on the mini power tool. Use the same method of plunging as detailed above, that is, by placing one edge of the base plate in contact with the surface while the other is raised to keep the bit free. Lower the raised edge to insert the bit into the workpiece.

3–58. Follow the inscribed edge of the shape as accurately as possible and clear all the waste from the recess with a disciplined action.

3–57. The diameter of the bit will depend on the shape and size of the inlay. Small-diameter bits follow curves easily, but can also be difficult to control and make a smooth edge. Larger-diameter bits of more than ³⁄₁₆th inch (4 mm) produce smoother curves, but create more drag and cannot produce tight curves.

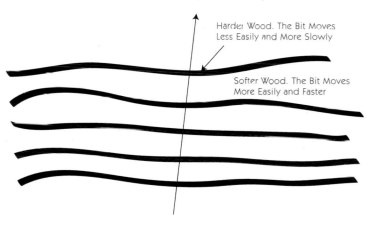

Harder Wood. The Bit Moves Less Easily and More Slowly

Softer Wood. The Bit Moves More Easily and Faster

3–59. When routing wood with a pronounced grain, care must be taken to avoid the effect of the varying hardness of the grain from causing the bit to deviate from its path. When cutting across the grain, the movement from harder to softer wood may cause the router to lurch forward as it meets less resistance.

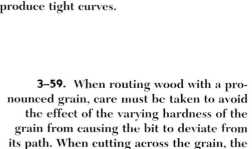

3–60. When you are cutting almost parallel to the grain, the harder areas will steer the bit to try to follow the line of the grain. Proceed with care in such situations.

3–61. Providing the marked outline has been followed fastidiously, the inlay should fit correctly and level with the surface. Glue should be applied to the recess and the inlay should be inserted immediately. If the glue is applied to the inlay and any time elapses before inserting it, there is the risk of the fibers swelling and deforming it, preventing a proper fit in the recess.

3–62. A small hammer is used, not to strike the inlay but to bring pressure to bear in small areas at a time to be sure of contact over the whole area.

3–63. Later when the glue is set, lightly rubbing over the inlay with a fine abrasive will finish the job.

USING PIN-GUIDED BITS

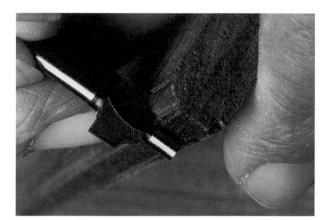

3–64. Some router bits have a central bearing; these are called pin-guided bits. In this case, the fence is not necessary because the pin rests against the edge of the workpiece and keeps the cutting edge a fixed distance from the edge. Pin-guided bits can be used only to cut recesses on the edge of a piece, and cannot be used to cut grooves in the center of a panel. Care must be taken not to press the pin too firmly against the edge; otherwise, the rapidly rotating pin may scorch the wood or score the surface.

3–65. The router base is used without a fence to produce a decorative edge molding. The pin-guided bit can be used on curved edges because it does not rely on a fence.

THE ROUTING TABLE

The routing table is useful for smaller workpieces because the work is taken to the router, rather than the router to the work, as with the router attachment. The mini power tool is mounted in the table with the bit facing up and protruding through a hole in the table. In **3–66 to 3–80**, the router table is being used to cut a groove in a wooden workpiece; in **3–81 to 3–85**, to trim; and in **3–86 to 3–88** to cut decorative moldings.

CUTTING GROOVES USING A ROUTER TABLE

3–66. Choose a bit with the equivalent diameter to the width of groove required. A bit can cut a wider groove than its diameter if multiple cuts are made. Fitting router bits is the same as fitting a drill bit. One of the major concerns is the installation of the shank fully into the collet as far as it will go. This is especially necessary because routing operations frequently involve side cutting that produces considerable lateral pressure on the collet and bearings of the mini power tool.

3–67. Be especially sure of tightening the collet nut securely.

3–68. Complete the bit installation by applying extra torque with the wrench.

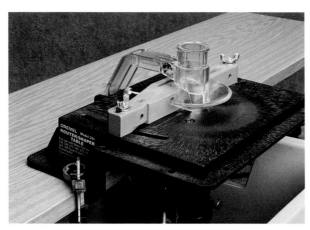

3–69. This is a typical router table setup, with the router table clamped to a work surface for security. For a more permanent setup, the table may be screwed to a piece of wood that may then be clamped to a bench.

3–70. Insert the mini power tool into the router table clamps using the collar or nose adapters as necessary and making sure that the shaft lock is accessible.

3–71. Remember to tighten the screws on both clamps.

3–73. Use the adjusting screw to set the bit height while checking the projection of the bit above the level of the table. Once this has been adjusted, tighten the clamps on the column.

3–72. Unlock the height adjustment on the mini power tool holder.

3–74. The height set.

Out-Feed Fence   In-Feed Fence

3–75. The fence consists of two parts: the in-feed side, which supports and guides the work as it is fed to the bit, and the out-feed side, which supports the work after it has left the bit.

3–76. Set the in-feed side to give the correct position for the groove in the workpiece. Setting of the out-feed side will depend on the depth of cut being made. In this case they will be level, because the workpiece remains the same distance from the fence on both sides of the cutter. Shown here is the adjustment of the in-feed side of the fence.

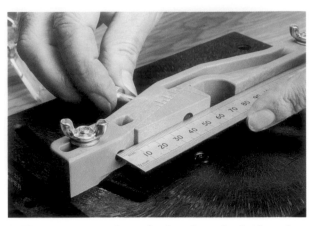

3–77. Comparing the in-feed and out-feed sides of the fence.

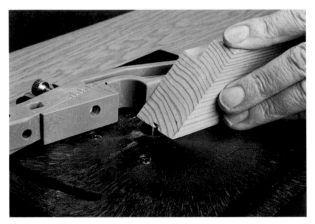

3–78. Cutting a groove with the out-feed side set to the same level as the in-feed side.

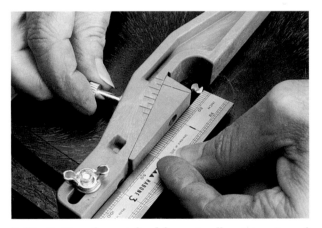

3–79. Setting the out-feed fence to allow trimming of the workpiece. The out-feed setting will be the same distance from the in-feed side as the depth of cut produced by the cutter.

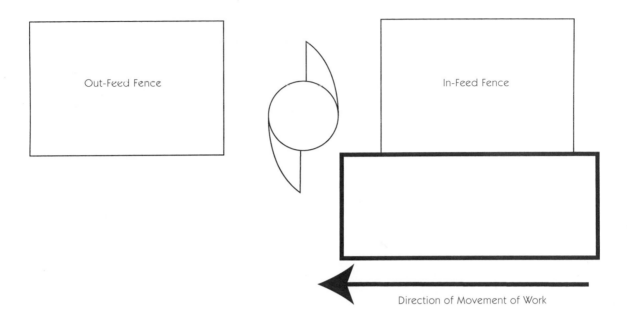

Out-Feed Fence

In-Feed Fence

Direction of Movement of Work

3–80. In previous examples of routing, the mini power tool has been held vertically with the bit pointing downward. When installed in a router table, the mini power tool is, as it were, upside down, that is, with the bit pointing up, through the table. The principle of movement of the bit related to the material as described in Cutting Grooves Along Edges still applies, but in this case the material is taken to the bit and it is now inverted. Looking down on the cutter, it will revolve counterclockwise; therefore, to apply the technique correctly the workpiece must move from right to left.

TRIMMING WITH A ROUTER TABLE

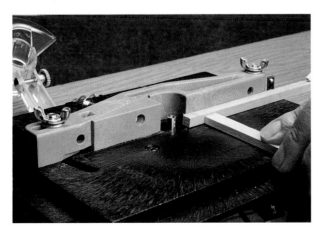

3–81. Trimming off a rough edge.

3–82. Using a push stick to keep work in contact with the fence during the whole routing operation.

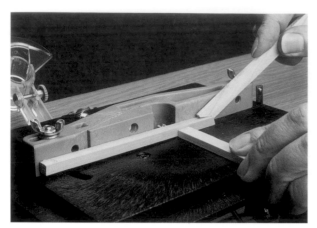

3–83. Using a push stick to feed the workpiece and keep fingers clear.

3–84. The trimming operation nearly completed.

3–85. Previous photos have not shown guards, for clarity of illustration; guards should be used whenever possible and in accordance with the manufacturer's instructions.

DECORATIVE MOLDINGS WITH A ROUTER TABLE

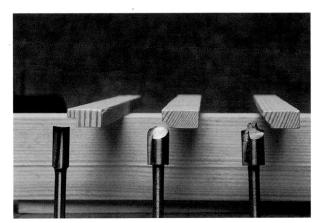

3–86. Shaped router bits can be used in a router table to produce decorative moldings on thin strips. These can be used for doll's houses and other craft projects.

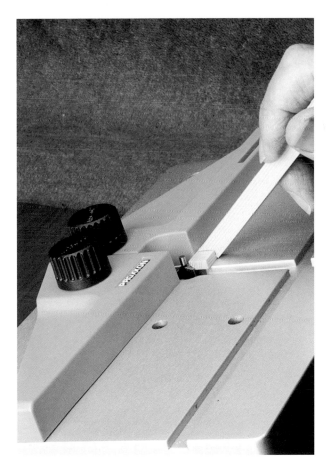

3–87. A push stick is used for safety and security to keep the work pressed closely against the fence and to push the work across the rotating bits. Moldings can be produced on the side of the work.

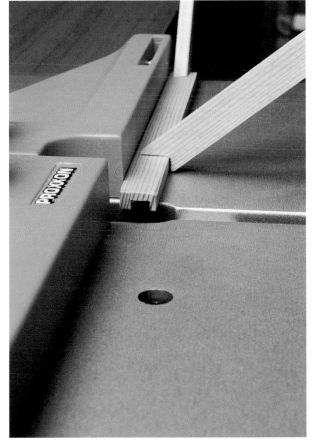

3–88. Alternatively, the cut may be made in the center of the workpiece to form a channel.

SAWING & CUTTING
TECHNIQUES

A range of attachments and cutter types are available to facilitate sawing and cutting operations depending on the type of job at hand. The small circular-saw blade or cutting disc is best suited for freehand work. Saw blades are relatively thin and appropriate for cutting wood (4–1), although some diamond-coated blades are available for cutting stone and metal (4–2). Cutting discs (4–3) are somewhat thicker than saw blades and are used to cut metal, ceramics, and stone. Lubrication may be required when cutting these materials.

It should be noted here that the oft-recommended practice of using a drill stand to hold cutter blades could pose considerable danger to the user. The lack of guards and the tendency for the material to be snatched and dragged into the cutter make this a potentially dangerous practice and it is recommended that the router table with its guards and fences be used instead.

The illustrations in this section show techniques for assembling the blade or cutting disc and arbor (pages 74 to 76) and using a cutting disc (pages 76 and 77).

BLADES AND CUTTING DISCS

4–1. Circular saw blades.

4–2. Diamond-coated blades such as this one can be used to cut stone and metal. In the background is shown an arbor to which it will be attached.

4–3. Cutting discs can be used to cut metal, ceramics, and stone.

ASSEMBLING THE BLADE OR CUTTING DISC AND ARBOR

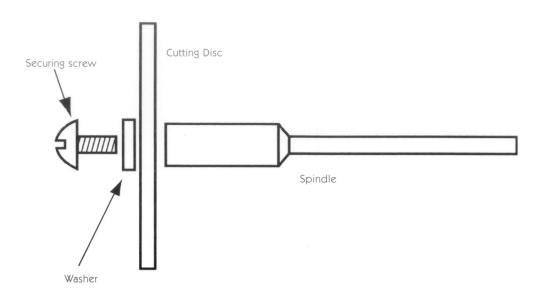

Securing screw

Cutting Disc

Spindle

Washer

4–4. This diagram shows an arbor assembly. An arbor is a spindle to which may be attached a circular-saw blade or cutting disc by means of a retaining screw and washer. The plain end of the spindle is held in a chuck, or collet, of the mini power tool.

4–5. To assemble the saw and arbor, first remove the securing screw and washer and insert the spindle in the chuck or collet. This example shows a chuck being used. The spindle should be inserted fully into the chuck.

4–6. Tighten the chuck or collet to secure the spindle.

Direction
of Rotation

4–7. Insert the screw, with the washer attached, into the central hole in the saw blade. Make sure that the washer is placed between the screw head and the saw blade. See that the teeth on the blade face in the direction shown when viewed from the screw side. If a cutting disc is used as an alternative to the saw blade, either way round will do, as there are no teeth on a cutting disc.

4–8. Insert the screw carrying the washer and saw blade into the threaded hole in the end of the spindle.

4–9. With a screwdriver of the correct size, tighten the screw in the spindle to hold the saw blade firmly. Be careful to see that the saw blade will not slip, but try not to use excessive force as this might damage the components.

4–10. A vise is used to hold the workpiece securely and safely away from possible contact of the saw blade with the hands. Sawing may be commenced with the saw held at a constant angle and applied with steady downward pressure without force. If the blade slips, remove it carefully, switch off the mini power tool, and tighten the retaining screw. Start up the mini power tool again and reapply the saw blade carefully.

4–11. As the sawing operation is being performed, hold the mini power tool steady, trying to keep the saw blade in line with the cut and not twisting it. Any movement away from the saw line is likely to cause binding, resulting in possible damage to the workpiece or the saw blade.

4–12. A clean cut is the reward.

SAWING WITH A CUTTING DISC

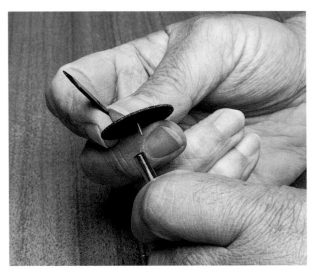

4–13. Circular-cutting discs are made from solid abrasive materials. They are used to cut metal, stone, and ceramics. Cutting discs vary slightly in thickness, but they are generally thicker than circular-saw blades. They are mounted on an arbor in the same way as the saw blade and used in exactly the same manner.

4–14. Cutting discs can be used to cut composite materials, for example plastic-coated cables and rusty bolts, and even hardened metals such as chain links. In this case, a bolt is being cut to the required length.

4–15. It is important not to use the cutting disc on the side (like a sanding disc), as shown here, because the side pressure on the brittle disc will cause it to break and throw particles outward at great speed.

ACCESSORIES DEDICATED TO SAWING OPERATIONS

Saw Table

The saw table is well suited to cutting thin strips or sheets and can easily maintain a straight cut and square edges. Illus. **4–16 to 4–24** demonstrate how to set up a saw table. Illus. **4–25 to 4–33** depict cuts that can be made with a saw table.

SETTING UP THE SAW TABLE

4–16. Minicraft saw-table parts.

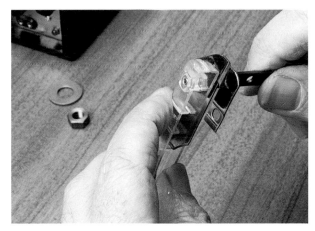

4–17. The riving knife and saw guard are a combined assembly. The riving knife is used to keep the kerf (the saw cut) open as the material passes the blade, thus preventing the material from closing up the saw slot and jamming on the blade. After the riving knife and guard are assembled, the lower tab on the riving knife is inserted through a slot in the saw table.

4–18. Use the small screw provided to secure the bracket to the underside of the saw table.

4–19. Use a small screwdriver to tighten the screw.

4–20. The blade is placed onto the spindle with its top edge protruding through the saw slot in the table and secured using the washer and nut.

Direction
of Rotation

4-21. It is important to fit the teeth on the saw blade to face in the direction as shown—that is, counterclockwise as one looks at the face of the saw blade when fitted.

4-22. Hold the spindle firmly with a wrench and use a second wrench to tighten the nut.

4-23. The blade protrudes through the slot in the top of the table and is kept safely covered by the guard. On the left is shown the cover that protects the lower part of the blade below the table.

4-24. The cover is pressed into place below the small locating lugs and slid down to lock it in position. If cutting metal with an abrasive disc or diamond-impregnated wheel, this cover may be filled with water or some other lubricant.

MAKING ANGLED CUTS WITH A MITER GUIDE

4–25. Angled cuts may be repeated accurately with this miter guide applied in combination with the parallel groove incorporated in the table surface. It is adjusted by loosening the locking knob and twisting the guide until the pointer is alongside the required angle.

4–26. When the pointer is aligned correctly, the knob is tightened.

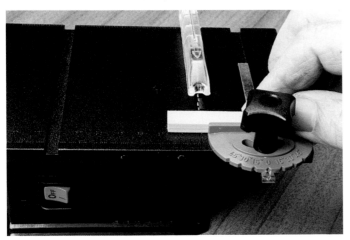

4–27. The base of the guide is located in the slot in the saw-table surface, such that the guide is free to slide forward. The material is placed so that it rests against the small fence of the guide. In this setting, it is possible to make right-angled cuts.

4–28. Use the speed controller to adjust the speed as suggested in the chart on pages 139 and 140.

4–29. Push the guide forward so the blade moves through the material smoothly. Keep a rate of feed such that the blade neither slows down excessively nor burns the workpiece.

4–30. In a similar manner, angled cuts can be made. In this case, the miter guide has been set to 45 degrees.

4–31. A square frame has been created using this method to cut 45-degree miters at each end of the four sides.

CUTTING STRIPS FROM A PANEL

4–32. To cut strips from a panel, the fence is used. This is secured parallel to the blade, using the locking knob or a small screw at the front. In practice, it was found that the line of approach by the workpiece was impeded by the locking knob provided, so it was changed in favor of a small screw.

4–33. When cutting thin strips, beware of catching fingers in the blade and use a small length of wood as a push stick, as shown in the left hand. Also, the use of a similar push stick to press the workpiece firmly against the fence is recommended (see the right hand). This latter push stick prevents the workpiece wandering away from contact with the fence and resulting in an uneven width of cut.

- - - - - - - - - - - - - - -

Jigsaws

Small jigsaws are capable of cutting both straight lines and curved shapes, and are best suited to cutting thin material—wood less than 5/16 inch (10 mm) and metal less than 1/8 inch (3 mm).

Illus. **4–34 to 4–48** show how to set up and use a jigsaw. Illus. **4–49 to 4–65** demonstrate miscellaneous cutting techniques.

SETTING UP AND USING A JIGSAW

4–34. Shown is a typical miniature jigsaw. It has a transformer that supplies the power from a main-circuit supply and allows speed control using the dial on the front panel.

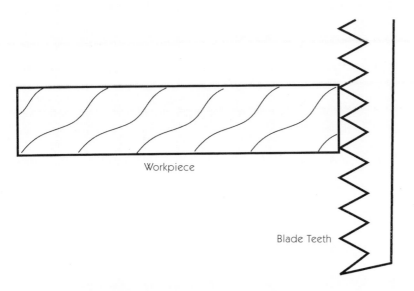

Workpiece

Blade Teeth

4–35. The next step is to insert the blade into the jigsaw, but first it must be determined which type to use. Blades are selected on the basic of material type and thickness. The material cut is usually either wood or metal. When selecting a blade, ensure that the teeth are arranged such that at least three teeth are in contact in the thickness of the material.

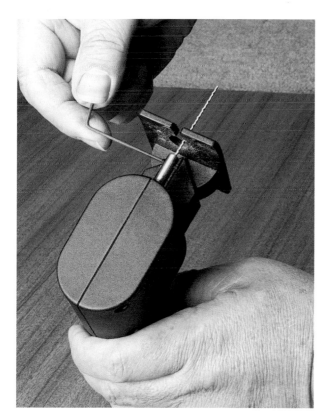

4–36. To change a blade in the jigsaw, first disconnect the unit from the power source and release the blade-holding screw with the Allen wrench.

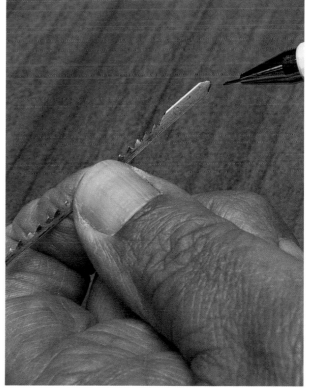

4–37. The blade has a flat section without teeth at the top. This end is inserted into the blade clamp for gripping.

4–38. Insert the flat section of the blade into the blade holder.

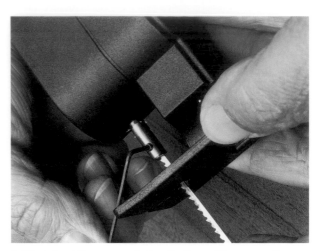

4–39. The Allen wrench (an L-shaped hexagonal metal bar) supplied is used to secure the blade in the blade holder.

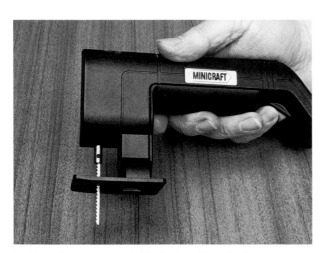

4–40. The jigsaw with blade fitted ready for use.

4–41. When using a jigsaw, it is essential to clamp the material being cut to a firm surface with sufficient clearance below the material for the blade to move up and down. Be sure that the cutting line does not overlap the support surface or the blade will cut in this also.

4-42. Set the speed to the recommendation in the chart on pages 139 and 140 and, with the workpiece firmly secured (here a vise is being used to hold strips of material), rest the base plate onto the work surface. Then start the jigsaw and gently guide the reciprocating blade forward to cut the material. The line to be followed can be seen through the gap in the base plate, ahead of the blade.

4-43. Continue to push gently forward as the cut proceeds, always keeping the base resting firmly on the surface of the workpiece; otherwise, the blade may jam in the cut.

4-44. Other types of jigsaw are set up in a similar manner.

4-45. While making the cut, it is possible to vary the direction by carefully guiding the mini power tool to follow, for example, a curved line.

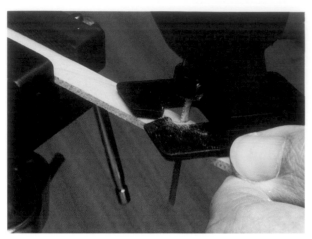

4–46. If the curve contains too small a radius, it is possible that the blade will jam in the saw slot. This would most likely lead to damage, even breakage, to the blade.

4–47. The smaller the width of the blade, measured from front to back, the smaller the radius that can be cut. The thickness of the blade also plays a part, as does the width of the teeth. These vary from one supplier to another and the only sure way to know the limits of the blade is to experiment carefully with waste material.

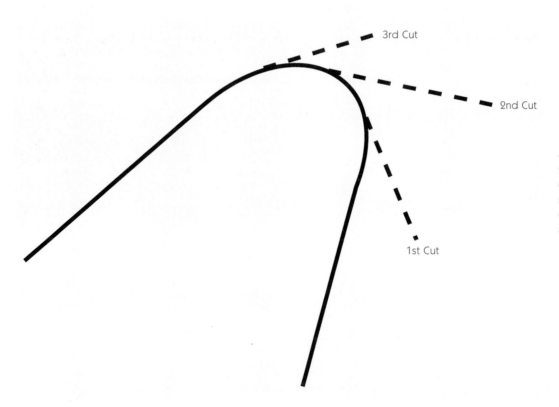

3rd Cut

2nd Cut

1st Cut

4–48. To cut tighter curves, a series of cuts can be made as shown.

CUTTING SHARP CORNERS

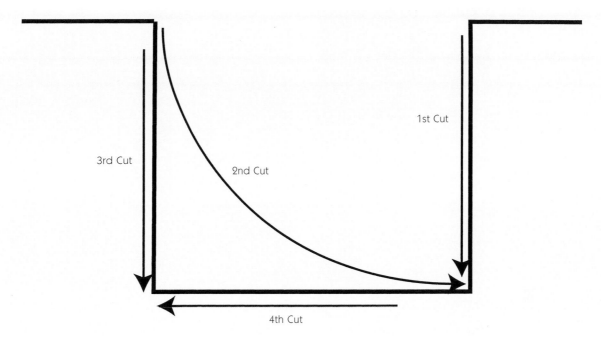

4–49. Although the saw is suited to sweeping curves, sharp corners can be achieved by using the technique shown in 4–50 to 4–55. Follow the order of cut from 1 through 4. The order of cuts for 3 and 4 are interchangeable.

4–50. Cutting sharp corners. A straight cut is made from the edge to the first corner. This is cut #1.

4–51. The cut looks like this.

4–52. The second cut is a curved one and is made from the second line to the first...

4–53. ...resulting in the cutout shown.

4–54. Two straight cuts (# 3 and 4) are then made into the second corner to clean up the cut...

4–55. ...producing a cutout with sharp corners rather than curves.

CUTTING HOLES IN THE CENTER OF A PANEL

4–56. The jigsaw can also be used to cut holes in the center of a panel. First select a drill bit slightly larger than the width of a blade.

4–57. Drill a hole in the waste area of the marked-out hole.

4–58. Insert the blade into the hole...

4–59. ...and proceed to cut out the hole...

4–60. ...until the waste is removed and the hole is revealed.

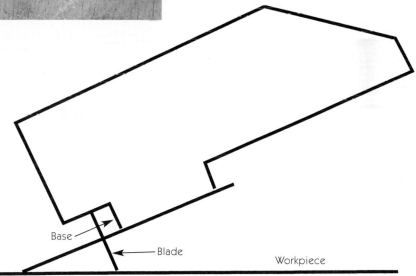

Base

Blade

Workpiece

4–61. With larger jigsaw machines, it is possible to plunge the blade into the workpiece by resting the base on the surface and gradually inserting the blade as it oscillates. Such a method should not be attempted with the mini power tool, however, because the small and slender blade is not strong enough and would certainly break under this kind of stress.

CUTTING MITERED PIECES

4–62. The base plate of the saw may be angled in order to cut mitered or angled pieces. The securing bolt is loosened with a screwdriver so that the base plate may be angled.

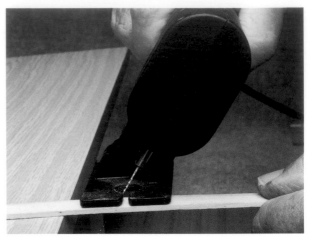

4–64. The cut is made as usual, keeping the base plate in firm contact with the surface...

4–63. After the base plate is angled, the bolt should be retightened.

4–65. ...to create an angled or beveled cut.

FLEXIBLE DRIVES

For many operations, such as engraving and carving, a flexible drive is of great advantage. It consists of a cable within an outer sleeve. One end of the cable is attached to the spindle of the mini power tool and the other end has a hand piece with a collet. The inner cable is rotated by the mini power tool spindle and thus rotates any cutter or drill bit that is installed in the collet.

The advantage of using a flexible drive is that it is much lighter than a mini power tool and therefore puts less strain on the user's hands and fingers. Also the hand piece is shaped more like a pen or stylus, which makes it easier to control for fine or detailed work. The disadvantage is that many types of hand piece can get rather hot and,

although a glove may be worn for protection, the discomfort of the hot tool limits the length of use at any one time.

Two types of flexible drive are available: those that attach to a mini power tool and those that combine a cable-and-motor unit. The latter types often incorporate a foot-operated speed control.

Illus. **5–1 to 5–7** show how to attach a flexible drive to a mini power tool. Illus. **5–8 to 5–15** depict assembly techniques for the stand that suspends the mini power tool above the workbench. Illus. **5–16 and 5–17** show the attachable flexible drive in use, and **5–18 to 5–35** show the setup and use of a dedicated flexible drive.

ATTACHING A FLEXIBLE DRIVE TO A MINI POWER TOOL

5–1. The attachment type of flexible drive.

5–2. To attach the flexible drive, it is necessary to remove the mini power tool collar and the collet nut.

5–3. Replace the collet with the drive adapter.

5–4. Tighten it into position.

5–5. Put the end of the flexible drive over the drive adapter.

5–6. Screw the end of the drive onto the collar thread.

5–7. The shank of the cutter, or drill bit, is then inserted into the hand-piece end of the flexible drive.

STAND ASSEMBLY TECHNIQUES

5–8. The mini power tool is suspended above the workbench by means of a stand. This is sold separately as a set of parts as shown. A bench clamp holds the tubes vertically; at the top of the bench clamp a hook is fitted. Most mini power tools have a wire loop to allow their suspension from this hook.

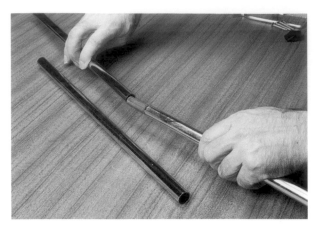

5–9. The tubes are first slotted into each other.

5–10. A hole in the bench clamp is available to hold the bottom end of the tube assembly.

5–11. A plastic insert is fitted into the top of the tubing.

5–12. The hook is installed into the plastic insert.

5–13. Using the clamp incorporated in the base, the assembly is attached to the edge of the work top.

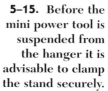

5–14. The stand's height can be adjusted either by using a different number of sections of pole or by varying the position of the poles in the clamp.

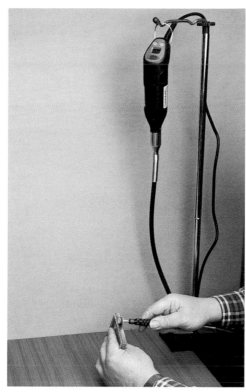

5–15. Before the mini power tool is suspended from the hanger it is advisable to clamp the stand securely.

USING AN ATTACHABLE FLEXIBLE DRIVE

5–16. The flexible drive is particularly good at working in tight spaces, for example, inside an object.

5–17. Because of the smaller body of the hand piece, a cut can be made in the center of a panel while keeping the cutter perpendicular. Compare the same application with the larger-bodied mini power tool, where the blade is not perpendicular to the surface.

SETTING UP AND USING A DEDICATED FLEXIBLE DRIVE

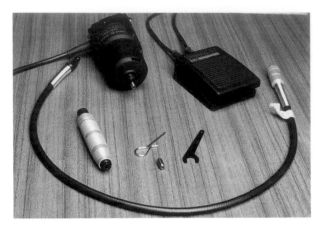

5–18. Dedicated flexible drives are available that include a foot switch/speed controller that allows greater precision. Because the hand piece contains a ball race, it is less likely to run hot after continuous use.

5–19. The heavy-duty motor unit has instead of a shaft lock a pin inserted through the collar and shaft to prevent rotation. Never perform this operation with the power unit connected to the main circuit.

5–20. The end of the flexible-drive cable is connected to the shaft.

5–21. It is tightened firmly in place. It need only be hand tight, as the direction of rotation will tend to tighten the connection rather than loosen it.

5–22. The collar of the outer cable is then connected to the collar of the power unit and tightened to finger tight.

5–23. The other end of the flexible cable is inserted into the hand piece.

5–24. It is pushed firmly until a secure click is heard...

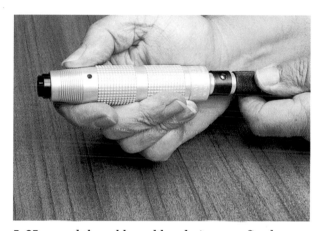

5–25. ...and the cable and hand piece are firmly connected.

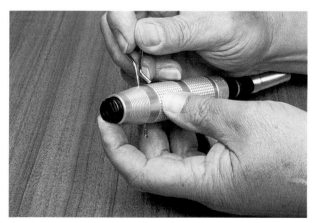

5–26. The locking pin is used through the hand piece to lock the shaft.

5–27. This allows a small wrench to be used to loosen the collet nut.

5–28. The nut is removed to expose the collet jaws.

5–29. Collet jaws of various diameters may be used.

5–30. To reassemble the collet, the collet nut is replaced.

5–31. It should be secured loosely with the fingers.

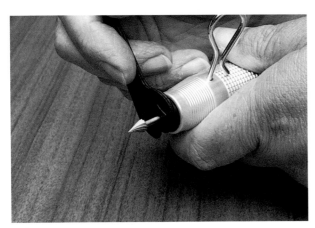

5–32. After inserting a drill bit or cutter, it can be tightened using the wrench.

5–33. Using the hand piece like a pencil gives excellent control over the movement of the tool, making the flex drive ideal for fine work, such as carving.

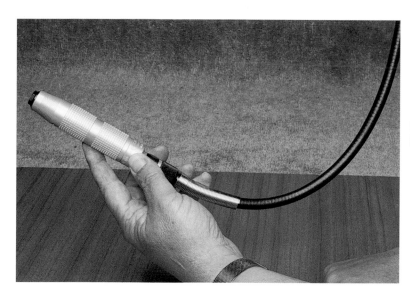

5–34. In use, the cable should be kept in a smooth curve.

5–35. If the curve is too small a radius, an unreasonable strain will be put on the components of the cable, resulting in increased wear and premature failure of the parts.

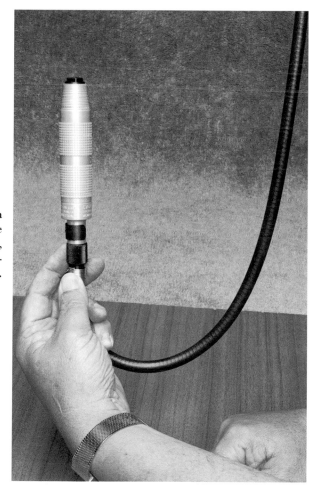

six

SHAPING & SMOOTHING

Mini power tools are well suited to a variety of shaping tasks, and a wide range of cutters and sanding accessories are available. Abrasive cutters are those that do not have teeth or cutting edges as with metal rotary blades or bits, but are made of an abrasive composition such as Carborundum or other synthetic material. Sanding drums and discs (**6–1**) are convenient for smoothing wood and metal. High-speed cutters (**6–2**), also known as rasps and burrs, can be used for rough shaping.

Illus. **6–3 to 6–11** show how to attach and use a sanding drum, and **6–12 and 6–13** how to use a flap wheel. Illus. **6–14 to 6–22** depict disc-sanding techniques.

Rasps and burrs are discussed on pages 106 and 107.

6–1. Sanding drums and discs.

6–2. High-speed cutters (also known as rasps and burrs).

ATTACHING AND USING A SANDING DRUM

6–3. The sanding drum consists of a cylinder of rubbery resilient material over which an abrasive sleeve is secured. Select the abrasive to match the work to be done. A coarse abrasive will remove material quickly; a fine abrasive removes material more slowly and leaves a finer finish. Usually the abrasives are supplied in packs of various grades. Start with a coarser grade and work toward a finer grade.

6–4. To attach the abrasive sleeve to this type of drum, the screw is first loosened to reduce the diameter of the drum. The abrasive sleeve is then mounted on the drum so that it covers the whole surface of the cylinder.

6–5. Do not allow any abrasive to overhang the end of the drum.

6–6. Retighten the screw to expand the drum segments and secure the abrasive sleeve.

6–7. This type of drum uses the flexibility of the segments to hold the abrasive cylinder, and the abrasive only needs to be pushed firmly in place.

6–8. The sanding drum is pushed onto the carrier.

6–9. Insert the spindle of the drum into the collet of the mini power tool and tighten the collet nut securely.

6–10. The smoothing of curves is an example of a freehand application of the abrasive drum.

6–11. In many cases, there is a benefit, including that of safety, in using a vise to hold the workpiece. Here the drum cylinder is held parallel to the surface to prevent the edges of the drum digging in and causing grooves. Do not press too hard; otherwise, a dip or hollow may be formed in the work. For heavier applications, it is better to secure the vise with screws or clamps.

USING A FLAP WHEEL

6–12. For surface smoothing, an alternative to the abrasive drum is the flap wheel. This consists of a series of strips of abrasive cloth arranged like the blades of a propeller attached to a spindle. Because the strips are flexible, they adapt themselves to the surface with which they come into contact as they rotate. This avoids the need to keep the wheel parallel to the surface, as the strips are unlikely to dig in. The strips also beat at the surface, which tends to shake off dust particles and makes the flap wheel less likely to clog.

6–13. Apply the flap wheel to the surface of the workpiece using a stroking action. The direction of the stroke is best when applied in the same direction as the wheel is turning, for example, from the operator's viewpoint, from left to right. Because flap wheels are unlikely to dig in, they can be used on flat or curved surfaces.

DISC SANDING

6–14. Disc sanding is best applied to flat surfaces. Two types of disc sander are available: those whose discs are secured by a screw to an arbor (as shown here) and those whose discs have an adhesive backing and are attached to a flexible rubber pad.

6–15. For the type that is fastened to an arbor, secure the disc to the arbor using the screw and tighten it with a screwdriver.

6–16. The screw that is used to secure the disc to the arbor will not allow the whole disc to lie flat on the surface, so only one side of the disc may be applied at any time. Because this type of disc is not supported, it will be found that as the disc is applied the pressure distorts it. Thus, the mini power tool will have to be held at an angle to ensure a flat surface.

6–17. Be careful not to let the screw touch the surface or scratches will result.

6–18. Discs with adhesive backing are attached to a rubber pad by first removing the protective backing from the adhesive and aligning the disc with the rubber pad.

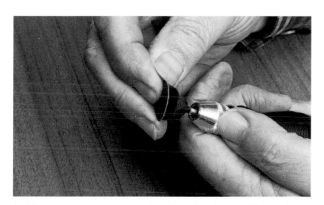

6–19. Firm pressure applied to the disc will attach it to the pad with sufficient security for sanding operations. Removal of the disc requires the lifting of one edge of the disc and peeling it off.

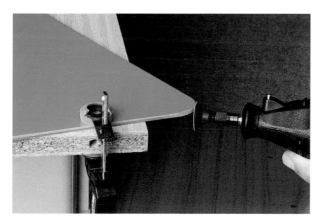

6–20. Again, mainly use one side of this disc, to avoid loss of control should the entire disc come into contact with the surface.

6–21. However, the design of the adhesive disc does allow it to be used flat on the material if a firm grip is used and only light pressure is applied.

6–22. If abrasive discs or drums become clogged with particles of wood dust, they may be cleaned by rubbing them against a piece of rubber or flexible plastic. An ordinary eraser may be used.

RASPS & BURRS

Wood can be carved by cutters made from high-speed steel (HSS) or tungsten carbide (TC). These cutters are also known as rasps and burrs.

Cutters of various shapes are available to help in producing fine detail (**6–23 to 6–26**). The tungsten-carbide cutters can also be used to cut metal and plastic.

RASPS AND BURRS

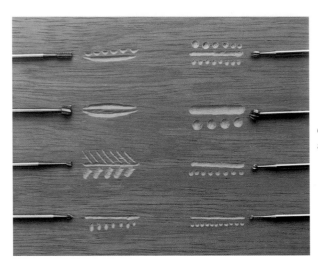

6–23. Different types of cutter create a variety of effects and the user is advised to experiment.

6–24. Small burrs can be used to define detail on carvings. As with all applications where a rotary cutter is involved, the direction of sweep of the cutter is critical. Best to experiment with a piece of waste material to acquire the feel of the tool and to judge which direction produces the best result. This operation is often easier using a flexible drive—either the attachment type or the separate unit. (Flexible drives are discussed in Chapter 5.)

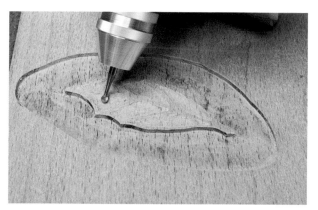

6–25. Typically, this type of cutter does not cut well on the tip, so the side should be used for best efficiency.

6–26. For rapid removal of material, the structured-tooth tungsten-carbide cutter can be used. It may also be used on soft metals. On hard metals, the teeth soon become worn.

DEDICATED UNITS

Disc-Sanding Table

This small, dedicated unit (**6–27 to 6–33**) consists of a rotating support disc coated with hook-and-loop material. An abrasive disc is coated with the same so the two will lock together when brought into contact.

SETTING UP AND USING A DISC-SANDING TABLE

6–27. To use this type of mini power tool, first select an abrasive disc of the appropriate grade—coarse for rapid removal of material and fine to produce a smooth finish. Then take the abrasive disc in the hands as shown.

6–28. With the machine switched off, place the abrasive disc so the center part contacts the support disc first.

6–29. Press the abrasive disc firmly on the support disc starting from the center and progressing to the outside. This ensures that the disc is held as flat as possible.

6–31. A miter guide can also be used with the sanding table. This is ideal for trimming or correcting workpieces prior to joining them together.

6–30. The support table slides onto the front of the unit. Two purposes are served by the support table: the workpiece is held firmly during the abrasive operation and the sanded face will be square to the table because of the right-angled orientation of the sanding disc. Viewed from the front, the disc revolves counterclockwise, so it is better to apply the workpiece to the left-hand side, because the tendency is for the disc to hold down the workpiece as it rotates. If the workpiece is held against the right-hand side, it would tend to lift it from the table.

6–32. Using the miter-guide fence to rest the workpiece against during the sanding operation will ensure that the end of the work is kept at right angles...

6–33. ...or at any angle desired. Here the workpiece is being mitered at 45 degrees.

Orbital Sander

The miniature orbital sander has an eccentric sanding motion that smoothes and flattens surfaces. Illus. **6–34 to 6–38** show sanding techniques using the type of abrasive that is attached to the orbital sander with securing clips. Illus. **6–39 to 6–48** show sanding techniques using abrasives that are attached to the orbital sander with a hook and loop.

SANDING WITH ABRASIVES SECURED WITH CLIPS

6–34. The miniature orbital sander is used to smooth and flatten surfaces. It rotates in an eccentric, or orbital, motion, allowing a smoothing action without the score marks associated with rotary disc sanders. The speed can be controlled by the power unit.

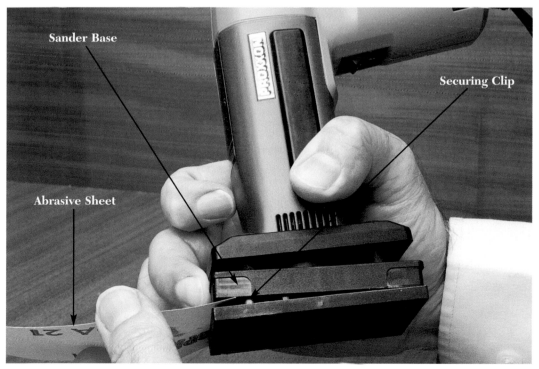

6–35. Select a suitable grade of abrasive. To apply the abrasive, hold it against the base of the sander, locating it symmetrically, and lift one of the securing clips. Tuck in one end of the abrasive sheet and release the clip so that it holds the end of the sheet.

6–36. Stretch the abrasive sheet across the base and, pressing down the other clip, ease the end of the sheet under the clip. When the clip is released, it should secure the end of the sheet.

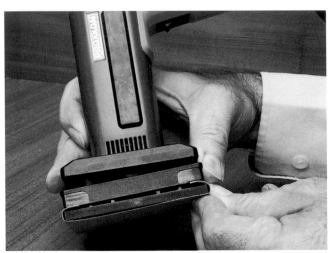

6–37. Check that the abrasive sheet is flat on the base and does not overhang at any part. Check that the curve of the paper from base to securing clip is taut.

6–38. Start the motor and place the sander flat on the surface. Move the sander forward and backward, following the direction of the grain. Work from coarser to finer grits of abrasive until the workpiece is sufficiently smooth. A faster speed will also result in a smoother finish and remove material faster.

SANDING WITH A HOOK-AND-LOOP ABRASIVE

6–39. The second type of attachment for the abrasive sheet is the use of a hook and loop (Velcro), similar to that described above for the disc-sanding table (refer to 6–29 to 6–35).

6–40. Take the abrasive sheet and locate it symmetrically on the base, pressing from center to edge to attach it to the base.

6–41. Apply the sander in exactly the same way as described for the type that uses spring-clip retention of the abrasive sheet.

6–42. Some systems have a curved base pad that can be used to sand concave or convex surfaces.

6–43. The pad is clipped onto the base.

6–44. The abrasive is secured by means of the clips at each end of the base. First it is inserted into one clip.

6–45. Then it is stretched across the pad and secured under the other clip.

6–46. The abrasive sheet should rest smoothly without creases on the pad with no overhang at the sides.

6–47. The foam pad will conform to concave surfaces...

6–48. ...or convex ones.

- - - - - - - - - - - - - - -

ROUTER TABLE

Illus. **6–49 to 6–56** show a router table set up and used for edge-trimming to an angle.

SETTING UP AND EDGE-TRIMMING WITH A ROUTER TABLE

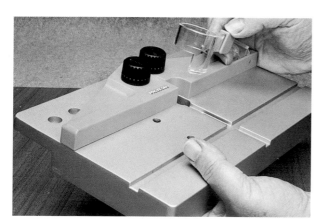

6–49. This router table may be used in sanding applications.

6–50. A clamping arrangement is provided for ease of location and attachment of the mini power tool. A cylindrical sanding drum has been fitted in the collet.

6–51. It is necessary to use a wrench to tighten the clamp screws to secure the mini power tool.

6–52. Setting the cutter to the required angle to trim the edge of the workpiece. The desired angle is achieved by adjusting the bracket to which the clamp is attached.

6–53. Here a burr is being used to trim the heart-shaped inlay.

6–54. A small drum sander is set at a slight angle to create a wedge-shaped section for close fitting of the inlay.

6–55. Movement of the workpiece is across the drum sander in the opposite direction of its rotation.

6–56. Smooth edges at a slight angle will help to achieve a precision fit of the inlaid heart.

chapter
seven

ENGRAVING
TECHNIQUES

Mini power tools can be used to engrave a variety of materials including glass, ceramics, metal, and stone. A wide variety of cutters is available. For engraving glass and stone, diamond points (**7–1**) are available; and for metal, tungsten carbide (**7–2**) may be used. Illus. **7–3 to 7–12** demonstrate techniques for engraving a design on glass. Illus. **7–13** shows a technique for engraving designs onto stone.

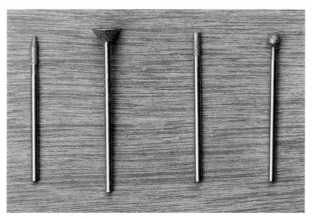

7–1. Diamond points.

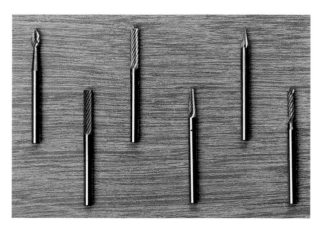

7–2. Tungsten-carbide cutters.

ENGRAVING A DESIGN ON GLASS

7–3. Engraving a design on glass. Any suitable design may be chosen and traced onto paper.

7–4. Adhesive tape is used to attach the tracing to the inside of the glass.

7–5. Either a flexible drive or a purposely made engraving tool is best for this job. For engraving operations, the flexible drive, if fitted with a hand piece, is desirable from several points of view: its on–off switch is conveniently placed under the finger, it has a foot-operated speed control, and the unit is lighter than the motorized mini power tool. The engraving bit is simply pushed into the collet of the engraver, where it is automatically secured.

7–6. Ensure the tool is pushed fully into the collet as far as it will go.

7–7. In this example, the use of the engraver is shown. The glass can be held in the hand or gently in a vise, padded with paper towels to avoid breaking it. The operator holds the switch in the "on" position with the index finger, and uses the engraving point to trace the outline of the design clearly visible through the glass. Goggles or safety glasses should be worn for protection against flying glass splinters.

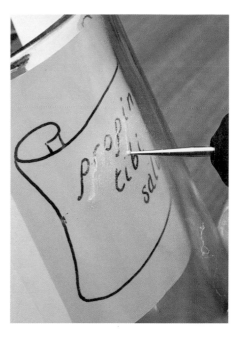

7–8. Interesting effects are possible cutting deeper for a thicker line, or lighter for a thinner one. Line thickness can also be varied by changing to a wider cutter...

7–11. Here a selection of cutters shows the different effects that can be created on glass. The user is advised to experiment on cutoffs of glass to see what effect can be achieved.

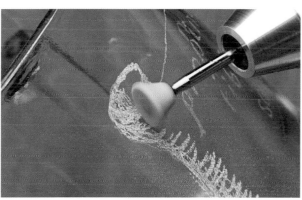

7–9. ...or by using the edge of an abrasive stone.

7–10. The result is a clean and clear design.

7–12. Variations can be achieved by using short strokes, deeper strokes, and different cutters or abrasive stones.

ENGRAVING DESIGNS ONTO BEACH PEBBLES

7–13. Designs can be engraved onto small beach pebbles. The normal engraving cutters will cut only soft stone and most beach pebbles are too hard for them. In this case, it is better to use an abrasive grinding point as shown.

eight

GRINDING
& POLISHING
TECHNIQUES

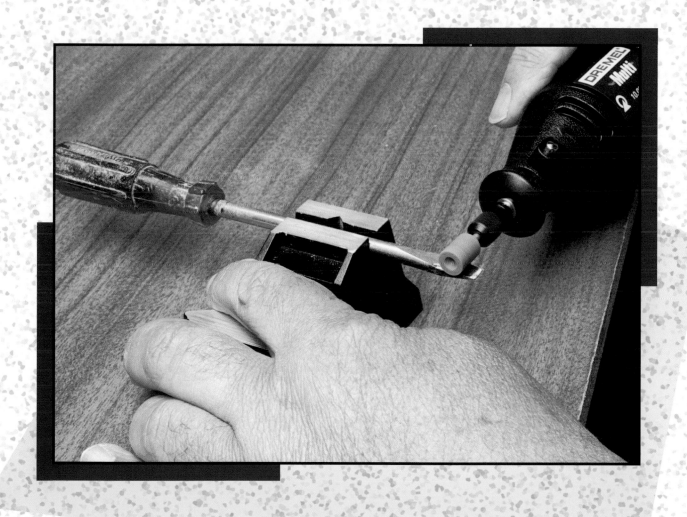

GRINDING

The grinding of metal is most commonly accomplished by the use of aluminum-oxide grinding points. Usually of a red/brown color, they are available in a variety of shapes as shown in **8–1 to 8–3**. Illus. **8–4 to 8–7** show some grinding-point uses.

ALUMINUM-OXIDE GRINDING POINTS

8–1. Aluminum-oxide grinding points.

8–2. The cylinder shape shown is a very useful general-purpose tool. It is made of an abrasive stone material and may be used for deburring and removing rough edges. Such tools are often referred to as "stones." Undesirable burrs often occur as a result of drilling holes in sheet metal, particularly on the underside of a drilling operation where the drill has broken through. Because of its right-angle edge, this stone is easier to use for such work.

Having set the mini power tool speed, apply the stone gently at first, moving constantly across the surface. On narrow work, try to use different parts of the stone's edge to prevent uneven wear. Such damage causes a groove or hollow in the surface.

8–3. This round cone is another helpful general-purpose stone. It is useful for sharpening various types of blade at various angles. For slender edges that need to be very sharp, use the part of the stone nearer the shaft (the finer angle), whereas for stronger edges, the part of the stone nearer the end is used.

GRINDING POINT USES

8–4. Examples of use: reshaping the end of a cut bolt. After cutting off a length of threaded rod or a bolt, it would be sensible to smooth the end to avoid the risk of personal injury. Applying the abrasive stone to the rough end of the bolt is a quick way to accomplish this.

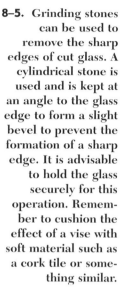

8–5. Grinding stones can be used to remove the sharp edges of cut glass. A cylindrical stone is used and is kept at an angle to the glass edge to form a slight bevel to prevent the formation of a sharp edge. It is advisable to hold the glass securely for this operation. Remember to cushion the effect of a vise with soft material such as a cork tile or something similar.

8–6. When a grinding stone is applied to metal, there is a tendency for the small particles of waste material to become embedded in the cavities in the surface of the stone. The softer the material being ground, the more likely it is to clog the stone. This reduces its efficiency to cut, making it necessary to clean away the embedded waste.

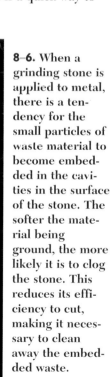

8–7. By applying a special piece of material called a "dressing stone" to the clogged surface, it will restore the stone to a nearly new condition. As the abrasive stone is rotating, the dressing stone is held in contact and moved across the surface. This action removes waste particles and a small layer of worn material from the abrasive stone surface. Smooth movement with even pressure is applied in order to create a uniform surface without grooves.

SHARPENING WITH GRINDING POINTS

Grinding points can be used to sharpen a variety of tools. Although too coarse to sharpen fine plane blade or carving tools, they are well suited to sharpening chisels, knives, scissors, shears, rotary mower blades that are not cylindrical, axes, and screwdrivers. These sharpening techniques are demonstrated in **8–8 to 8–14.**

SHARPENING VARIOUS TOOLS WITH GRINDING POINTS

8–8. Sharpening a chisel. As with other, similar applications of the mini power tool, it is best to secure either the workpiece or the machine. In this case, due to the need to control the angles and pressure with extreme care, it will be found suitable to grip the chisel in a vise and apply the mini power tool freehand.

Once a chisel has been given a sharp edge, it is a simple matter to resharpen without undue need to change the angle of the bevel. Best to begin by applying pressure at the top of the bevel (away from the sharp edge) and gradually lower the applied angle of the mini power tool. (The example shown here is a chisel-like blade.) This allows a progressive correction, if need be, as the operation proceeds. While the chisel is held in the vise, try cutting a piece of paper to test the edge for sharpness.

8–9. Sharpening a knife. Differing from chisels, knives have a long blade and are best applied free-hand to the mini power tool secured in a clamp or even in a drill stand. The angle of application is just as critical with knife blades as with chisels or any other blade used for cutting. It is all too easy to fall into the trap of increasing the angle for a quick fix of a blunt edge, but this is not recommended. The greater the angle at the edge, the more blunt it will be and the more metal that has to be removed to correct the error.

8–10. Sharpening scissors. Scissors should not have a knife edge, because they cut on a different principle, called "shearing." Each blade is ground to a little less than 90 degrees, and therefore does not seem to be sharp. This will be apparent if scissors are applied like a knife blade; they don't cut. It is the bringing together of the two blades wherein lies the cutting principle of scissors. In effect, the material being cut is squeezed between the blades until the edges meet and therefore sever the material. Try to maintain the original angle at which the scissors were ground.

Even if the scissors blades are not sharp as a knife blade, their edges must not be damaged or rounded.

Clamping either the scissors or the mini power tool is essential for safety and security.

8–11. Sharpening shears. Exactly the same principle must be applied to shears as with scissors. Since shear blades are so much bigger, it is best to use the largest grinding stone available for the mini power tool.

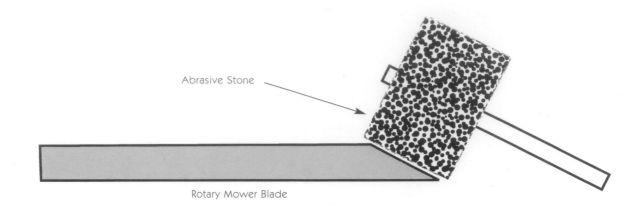

Abrasive Stone

Rotary Mower Blade

8–12. Rotary mowers, that is, the type of mowers with a pair of blades rotating horizontally (not the cylinder variety), may also be sharpened with a mini power tool. It is also possible with many brands to sharpen the blades without removal from the mower. However, it cannot be denied that it is worth the effort to remove the blades and clamp them securely to allow both hands to control the mini power tools.

    Mower blades become severely damaged by stones and other hard objects in the course of lawn trimming. Often the edges are rounded and almost smooth by wear or misuse. New edges are retrievable by some patient and disciplined care with the mini power tool fitted with a coarse abrasive stone. It is important once again to stress that the original angle should be maintained, assuming there is anything left of it!

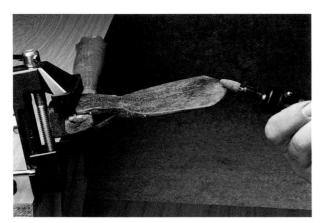

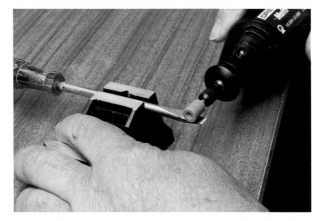

8–13. Sharpening an axe. This is another case of deciding whether to clamp the axe or the mini power tool. Assuming that a method of securing the axe is available, clamp it firmly and apply the mini power tool freehand.

    Coarse stones will be best for this job since some hefty corrective measures will probably be necessary. Axes do not need to be as sharp as knives or chisels but, nevertheless, the sharper they are, the more efficiently they will cut. And the less effort needed to swing the axe!

8–14. Sharpening a screwdriver. Much abused and seldom in good condition, the humble but essential screwdriver is a good friend when its blade is correctly formed. It is best always to try to use a screwdriver of the correct size to fit the screw.

    Normally, it is sensible first to grind away the front of the blade to remove any worn or rounded edges. If this means that the recovered edge is now too wide to fit into the screw slot, then some thinning down must be done. This should be achieved by removing a little from each side of the blade without changing the angle of the bevel.

SILICON-CARBIDE GRINDING STONES

Silicon carbide grinding stones are usually blue-green. They are finer and harder than aluminum-oxide stones and are intended for use on hard materials such as glass, stone, and ceramics. They can be used to remove material and to engrave designs onto the surface. A range of shapes is available as shown in **8–15**.

Silicon-carbide grinding stones of various point types create different effects, so the user should experiment on a cutoff piece of glass. In keeping with other abrasive and cutting operations, the direction of the cutting stroke is significant. In order to establish a technique, take a pen-hold grip applied with the stone resting on the surface of the workpiece. To stroke from right to left has a more positive, controlled feel to the action than is found if stroking in the opposite direction. This means that the rotary direction of the cutter will be traveling against the direction of the work surface.

8–15. Silicon-carbide grinding stones.

CLEANING AND POLISHING TECHNIQUES

Rotary Brushes

Rotary brushes can be used to clean a wide variety of materials. They are particularly useful for cleaning difficult-to-reach crevices on an object.

Brushes are made of four different types of material. Bristle brushes—recognized by their black color—are used for soft or precious materials such as may be found in jewelry or silverware. They can be used with a polishing compound and various proprietary brands are available for this purpose.

Steel (wire) brushes are excellent for removing rust or corrosion. They are used on harder metals such as iron and steel. Brass brushes, identified by their gold color, are softer than steel brushes and will not scratch soft metals such as brass, copper, or gold.

Stainless-steel brushes are used in cases where it is necessary to avoid leaving tiny particles behind embedded in the workpiece. With a brush made of common steel, such particles would rust eventually and cause discoloration. Use them on aluminum, pewter, and stainless steel.

Rotary brushes come in three main shapes: cup (**8–16 and 8–17**), pencil (**8–16 and 8–18**), and wheel (**8–16 and 8–19**). Illus. **8–20 and 8–21** show rotary brushes being used to clean grooves and threads.

Illus. **8–29 to 8–36** show the sequence involved in cleaning and polishing abalone shell.

ROTARY BRUSH SHAPES

8–16. There are three main shapes of rotary brush. They are, as shown from left to right, wheel, cup, and pencil shapes.

8–17. The cup-shaped steel brush can be used to clean inside objects just as this spokeshave. Usually one side of the brush is used, although the entire end can be used to contact the surface.

8–18. The pencil-shaped bristle brush is also used for inside objects or difficult-to-reach crevices.

8–19. The wheel-shaped steel brush is a good general-purpose shape for surface cleaning.

CLEANING GROOVES AND THREADS WITH ROTARY BRUSHES

8–20. Cleaning grooves.

8–21. Cleaning threads that are rusty or clogged.

POLISHING WITH CLOTH AND FELT WHEELS

8–22. A number of different types of polishing point and wheel are available that may be used on their own or with polishing compound.

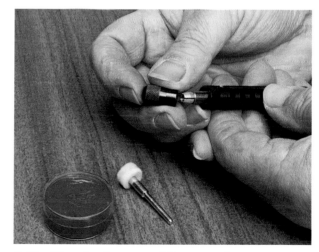

8–23. The wheels are used for general-purpose cleaning of flat or curved surfaces.

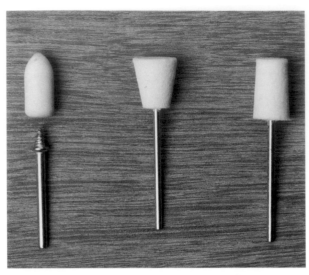

8–24. Felt-point shapes. These are firmer and can be used with greater pressure than cloth wheels, and can be used for polishing detail.

8–25. Cloth wheels are more suitable for a final buffing.

8–26. Felt wheels are supplied either on an integral arbor or fitted onto a screw mandrel, which is shown here.

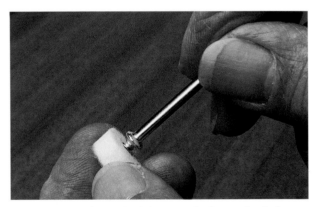

8–27. Insert the end of the mandrel into the hole in the center of the wheel and screw it into position.

8–28. Notice that these types of wheel are not as secure as those on integral arbors and are usually only suitable for lighter work.

CLEANING AND POLISHING SEQUENCE

8–29. A typical cleaning and polishing sequence will run through a series of stages, each using a different tool.

8–30. In this example, a piece of abalone shell is first cleaned with a wire brush to remove loose material. For these operations, a dust mask is essential because the shell dust is potentially harmful if inhaled.

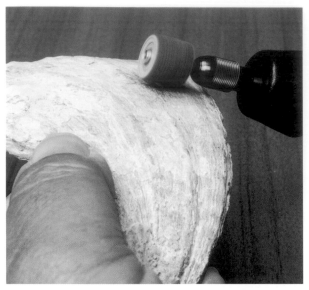

8–31. This is followed by a sanding drum to remove the softer outer layer of shell.

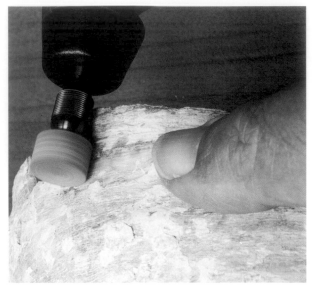

8–32. As the harder layers are reached, a grinding stone will be necessary to provide a smooth surface. It may be necessary to use two grades of stone or to use an older more worn stone for the final grinding as this will give a smoother finish.

8–33. The first polishing can use a polishing paste as shown. Only a small amount should be rubbed into the surface because the rotating "mop" will throw any excess in all directions. Beware that the paste will stain clothes.

8–34. The "mop" with paste should be moved evenly over the surface until a fine layer has been removed and the polished surface is beginning to show.

8–35. A final buffing should be done with a clean felt wheel.

8–36. This will result in a high-quality luster.

nine

TOOL CHARTS
& CUTTING
GUIDELINES

Table 1.

MINI POWER TOOL COMPARISON CHART							
	Power Supply	Power Rating	Speed Range (RPM)	Speed Control	Collet Supplied	Attachments Available	Note
Black & Decker Wizard RT550	Main Circuit	90W	8,000-27,000	Continuously Variable	Yes (Maximum Capacity .11 inch, 3 mm)	Yes (Bench Drill Holder, Flexible Drill, and Router Base)	Available as Kit with Accessories
Dremel 6V Cordless Engraver	4 Penlight Batteries			Two Speed	Yes (.09 and .12 inch, 2.4 and 3.2 mm)	No	
Dremel Heavy-Duty Flex Shaft	Main Circuit	250W	0 to 22,000	Foot Switch, Continuously Variable	Yes (.12 and .25 inch, 3.2 and 6.4 mm)	No	Available as Set with Accessories (Bench Drill Holder, Drill Stand, Flexible Drive, Router Base, and Router Table) and Storage Rack
Dremel Multi Cordless	Rechargeable		7,500 and 15,000	Two Speed	Yes (.12 inch, 3.2 mm)	No	Available as Set with Carry Case and Accessories
Dremel Multi 395	Main Circuit	125W	10,000 to 33,000	5 Steps	Yes (.12 inch, 3.2 mm	Yes (Bench Drill Holder, Drill Stand, Flexible Drive, and Router Table)	Available as Set 39950 with Carry Case and Accessories
Dremel Professional	Main Circuit	125W	5,000 to 33,000	Electronic in 1,000 rpm Steps	Yes (.12 inch 3.2 mm)	Yes (Drill Stand, Router Table, Router Base, Flexible Drive, and Bench Drill Holder)	Available as Set with Carry Case and Accessories

Mini Power Tool Comparison Chart (continued)

	Power Supply	Power Rating	Speed Range (RPM)	Speed Control	Collet Supplied	Attachments Available	Note
Minicraft MB1010	0-18V DC Separate Unit	100W	0-18,000	Continuously Variable On Power Supply	Chuck (.015 to 12 inch, 0.4 to 3.2 mm)	Yes (Drill Stand, Bench Drill Holder, Flexible Drive, Lathe)	Available as Kit with Accessories
Minicraft MB1012	0-18V DC Separate Unit	100W	0-18,000	Continuously Variable On Power Supply	Chuck (.015 to .12 inch, 0.4 to 3.2 mm)	Yes (Drill Stand, Bench Drill Holder, Flexible Drive, Lathe)	Available as Kit with Accessories
Minicraft MB170	0-188V DC Separate Unit	40W	0-30,000	Continuously Variable On Power Supply	Chuck (.015 to .12 inch, 0.4 to 3.2 mm)	Yes (Drill Stand, Bench Drill Holder, Flexible Drive, Lathe)	Available as Kit with Accessories
Minicraft MB150	0-18V DC Separate Unit	30W	0-30,000	Continuously Variable On Power Supply	Chuck (.015 to .12 inch, 0.4 to 3.2 mm)	Yes (Drill Stand, Bench Drill Holder, Flexible Drive, Lathe)	Available as Kit with Accessories
Minicraft MB130	0-18V DC Separate Unit	30W	0-30,000	Continuously Variable On Power Supply	3 Collets Supplied (.03, .06, and .09 inch, 1, 1.5, and 2.3 mm)	Yes (Bench Drill Holder, Drill Stand, Flexible Drive, Lathe)	Available as Kit with Accessories
Minicraft MB185 Engraving Pen	0-18V DC Separate Unit	6W	0-17,000	Continuously Variable On Power Supply	Collet(.09 inch, 2.3 mm)	No	Available as Kit with Accessories
Proxxon FBS 230/E	Main Circuit	100W	5,000-20,000	Continuously Variable	Chuck (.019-090 inch, 0.5-2.3 mm)	Yes (Drill Stand, Router Table, Router Base, Flexible Drive, and Bench Drill Holder)	Available as Kit with Accessories
Proxxon 220/E	Main Circuit	100 W	5,000-20,000	Continuously Variable	Chuck 6 Supplied (.039–.12 inch, 1-3.2 mm)	Yes (Bench Drill Holder, Drill Stand, Flexible Drive, Router Base, and Router Table)	Available as Kit with Accessories

Mini Power Tool Comparison Chart (continued)

	Power Supply	Power Rating	Speed Range (RPM)	Speed Control	Collet Supplied	Attachments Available	Note
Proxxon FBS 12/E	12-18V Separate Power Unit	100W	3,000-15,000	Continuously Variable	Chuck (.019-.01 inch, 0.5–3.2 mm)	Yes (Bench Drill Holder, Drill Stand, Flexible Drive, Router Base, and Router Table)	Available as Kit with Accessories
Proxxon GG12 Engraving Tool	12V Separate Power Unit	Approximately 6W	20,000	Fixed	Yes	No	Available as Kit with Accessories

Table 2.

DEDICATED UNIT COMPARISON CHART								
Make and Model	Power Supply	Power Rating	Speed Range (RPM)	Speed Control	Work Surface	Cutting Capacity	Blade Diameter	Notes
Minicraft MB410 Bench Saw	0-18V Separate Power Unit	100W	0-18,000	Continuously Variable on Power Unit	4.7 × 6.5 inches (119 × 169 mm)	Wood: .23 inch (6mm) Plastic: .08 inch (2 mm) Non-ferrous Metal: .04 inch (1 mm)	2.0 and 2.4 inches (50 and 60 mm)	Miter Guide Supplied
Minicraft MB55 Jigsaw	0-18V Separate Power Unit	100W	0-4,000 strokes/min.	Continuously Variable on Power Unit	.35 inch (9 mm)	Wood: 4 inches (10 mm) Plastic: .2 inch (5 mm) Non-ferrous Metal: .11 inch (3 mm)		Adjustable Bevel 45 to 90 Degrees

Dedicated Unit Comparison Chart (continued)

Make and Model	Power Supply	Power Rating	Speed Range (RPM)	Speed Control	Work Surface	Cutting Capacity	Blade Diameter	Notes
Minicraft MB450 Bench Disc Sander	0-18V Separate Power Unit	100W	0-18,000	Continuously Variable on Power Unit	Pad Diameter 3.0 inches (75 mm)			Miter Guide Supplied
Minicraft MB561 Orbital Sander	0-18V Separate Power Unit	100W	0-9,000	Continuously Variable on Power Unit	Pad Size 1.8 × 2.7 inches (48 × 68 mm)			
Proxxon STS12.E Jigsaw	0-18V Separate Power Unit	100W	2,000-5,000 strokes/ min	Continuously Variable on Power Unit		*Wood:* .4 inch (10 mm) *Plastic:* .11 inch (3 mm) *Non-ferrous Metal:* .10 inch (2.5 mm)		Cutting Stroke is ¼ inch (6 mm). There is no adjust-able bevel.
Proxxon SL12/E Orbital Sander	0-18V Separate Power Unit	100W	1,000-5,000	Continuously Variable on Power Unit	2.3 × 3.1 inches (58 × 80 mm)			Curved Surface Pad Avail-able

Table 3.

MATERIAL CUTTING GUIDELINES°							
Material		**Comments**	**Speed drilling**	**Speed routing**	**Speed sawing**	**Speed Engraving/ Grinding**	**Speed Shaping/ Carving**
Plastics	Acrylic PVS ABS	To avoid the tendency to clog the cutter or melt the material, a slow speed should be used. A lubricant or coolant applied to the cutting area is advised. Aggressive application may cause splintering of the material.	°°L	L	L	L	L
Natural Wood	Hardwood	Uneven grain or heavily figured wood can be troublesome.	M	M	M	N	M
	Softwood	Care is needed when crossing or when following the grain direction.	H	H	II	N	H
Man-Made Boards	MDF	Wear a dust mask because the dust is toxic.	H	H	II	N	H
	Chipboard	Some particles are harder than others and bonding resins present are tough. Difficult to produce a smooth surface from cutting operations.	M	M	M	N	N
	Hardboard	When drilling use a support block under the material being drilled and drill from the good side. Routers and other cutters tend to fluff up the cut edges.	H	H	H	N	N

Material Cutting Guidelines (continued)

Material		Comments	Speed drilling	Speed routing	Speed sawing	Speed Engraving/ Grinding	Speed Shaping/ Carving
	Plywood and Faced Veneer	Use a support block beneath any drilled areas to prevent tearout. Experiment to use the saw direction to damage the best side least.	M	M	M	N	M
Metal	Ferrous Brass Copper Aluminum	Use fluids such as soluble oils to lubricate and cool the cutter and the material during any machining operations. As with woods, the harder the material the slower the speed. (See note below on speeds.) It is important to prepare for drilling by marking the position of the hole with a center punch.	L	L	L	L	L
Other	Ceramics Glass Stone, Slate	Grinding operations are the most common with these materials and similar comments apply to each; high speeds are best with light strokes and take special care to wear protection for eyes and breathing.	L	N	N	H	H

*This table is intended to be used for general guidance.

**L=Low; M=Medium; H=High; N=Not recommended. Speed is part of an operational formula and depends on several variables, including the density of the material; the type of cutter being used; and the depth of cut being applied. These are variables that should be considered with each application, preferably after some trials using waste material.

Speed of rotation of the mini power tool spindle may not be adjustable on certain models, but usually they are connected to a transformer with a speed control. If not and the fixed speed is too fast for the recommended operation, it can be slightly compensated by the use of lighter strokes and shallow cuts with less aggression.

Remember always to check for advice on safety before operating any machine.

METRIC EQUIVALENTS CHART

Inches to Millimeters and Centimeters

MM=Millimeters   CM=Centimeters

Inches	MM	CM	Inches	CM	Inches	CM
⅛	3	0.3	9	22.9	30	76.2
¼	6	0.6	10	25.4	31	78.7
⅜	10	1.0	11	27.9	32	81.3
½	13	1.3	12	30.5	33	83.8
⅝	16	1.6	13	33.0	34	86.4
¾	19	1.9	14	35.6	35	88.9
⅞	22	2.2	15	38.1	36	91.4
1	25	2.5	16	40.6	37	94.0
1¼	32	3.2	17	43.2	38	96.5
1½	38	3.8	18	45.7	39	99.1
1¾	44	4.4	19	48.3	40	101.6
2	51	5.1	20	50.8	41	104.1
2½	64	6.4	21	53.3	42	106.7
3	76	7.6	22	55.9	43	109.2
3½	89	8.9	23	58.4	44	111.8
4	102	10.2	24	61.0	45	114.3
4½	114	11.4	25	63.5	46	116.8
5	127	12.7	26	66.0	47	119.4
6	152	15.2	27	68.6	48	121.9

INDEX